Donald MacIntosh is the eldest son of a Perthshire wood-cutter and a mother who hailed from the Wilderness Area of the Isle of Mull. He studied forestry in Argyll and worked with the Forestry Commission before spending the next thirty years as a tree prospector and surveyor in the rain-forests of Liberia, Ivory Coast, Gold Coast, Nigeria, Cameroon and Gabon.

During this time he lived with an astonishing hetero-geneity of tribes, from the Krahn elephant hunters of Liberia to the pygmies of West Central Africa. He had many encoun-ters with creatures great and small, from the lethal cobra and gaboon viper to the homicidal forest buffalo.

In the latter part of the 1960s, while the Biafran conflict was raging in West Africa, he lectured for three years on a variety of forestry-related subjects at a college in St John's, Newfoundland.

For the last few years he has been writing articles for a number of British and international magazines, mainly on subjects relating to the African rainforests. He has also writ-ten three books – *On the Mahogany Trail* (on rainforest tree species), *Travels in Galloway*, and *Travels in the White Man's Grave: Memoirs from West and Central Africa* (published by Abacus) which was shortlisted for the 1999 Thomas Cook Travel Book of the Year Award.

Forest of Memories
Tales From The Heart Of Africa

Donald MacIntosh

Little, Brown and Company

A *Little, Brown* Book

First published in Great Britain in 2001
by Little, Brown and Company

Copyright © Donald MacIntosh 2001

The moral right of the author has been asserted.

A CIP catalogue record for this book
is available from the British Library.

ISBN 0 316 85732 7

Typeset in Berkeley by M Rules
Printed and bound in Great Britain
by Clays Ltd, St Ives plc

Little, Brown and Company (UK)
Brettenham House
Lancaster Place
London WC2E 7EN

www.littlebrown.co.uk

For
Gordon and Katie Martin,
two long-time friends
and
fellow Old Coasters

Contents

'If a man does not keep pace with his companions, perhaps it is because he hears a different drummer. Let him step to the music he hears, however measured or far away.'

Henry David Thoreau

Preface

My whole life has revolved around trees. My earliest memory is of having tried to climb a large oak in the ancient Forest of Kilsture in Galloway, Scotland, at the tender age of four years. My boot got stuck in a cleft and it was some hours before I was found and rescued by my grandfather. I was not, it would appear, much put out by the inconvenience: it was springtime and the sun was shining, the joyful refrain of the chaffinch was carolling out through the green leaves above me, the forest floor was a shimmering sea of bluebells below, and I was perfectly comfortable sitting on my perch in the mossy fork of the tree.

We were living in an isolated cottage on the fringe of the forest at the time. My father, a woodcutter, had been assigned to the task of removing the mature trees in preparation for an extensive planting programme. I often went out with him to work, revelling in the steady, rhythmic

THUNK of his broad axe as it bit into the wood and the metallic singing of the great manual crosscut-saw wielded by him and the others when felling. Redundant branches and general tree litter were piled high on a roaring bonfire, and with each deposit, showers of gold and silver and orange sparks would erupt skyward to the fierce crackling of waxen leaves and the explosion of gummiferous pine blisters. It was a sight and a sound that never failed to induce within me a state of hypnotic fascination, and the heady fragrance of resin mingled with wood smoke remains with me to this day.

I studied forestry among the mountains of the Scottish Highlands, a suitably green and wet environment for what was to follow. For some reason inexplicable to me even now, I had always felt drawn to the rainforests of West and Central Africa, so at the end of my studies in the early 1950s when Unilever advertised for a qualified forester to join their ranks as a tree prospector and enumerator in their vast timber concessions along the Gulf of Guinea, I applied for the post. I was never to regret my decision.

Much of my work took me well away from the beaten track and therefore far from the company of other white people. Hitherto uncharted areas of forest had to be mapped in detail, and every species of tree above a certain minimum circumference plotted on those maps. It was necessary, therefore, to rapidly acquire an intimate knowledge of African tree species in order to be able to transcribe vernaculars supplied by one's tree-finders into such botanical names as might currently have been in existence. Also necessary was the ability to eat without flinching absolutely anything offered by the camp cook or the women in whose tiny villages one might have happened to be staying from time to time. I was lucky: I seemed to have been blessed with the digestive system of a Komodo dragon, for I drank water straight from the streams as my crew did without the usual prerequisite of having had it boiled, and I ate lumps of dried monkey meat so tough that only by virtue of the fact that they were riddled with maggot holes was it possible for any human being to chew his way through them. I was almost never sick. By the end of my first tour in Africa I had become a true 'bushman', as the inhabitants of the forest called themselves.

There were, of course, spells during the thirty years I spent in those rainforests when I found myself having to do some 'civilized' work for a change, such as helping to run a timber operation or grading logs for some shipping company or other. For a time, while Nigeria's civil war was grinding bloodily and inexorably onward, making work of any kind impossible, I even found myself teaching a variety of forestry-related subjects at a college in Newfoundland.

But the true wanderer is not readily shackled by the constraints of civilization. In the end, my thoughts could always be guaranteed to drift with mounting longing towards *my* people, my friends in those faraway lands and remote communities: the hunters, the fishermen, the subsistence farmers, the market women and the children with whom I had worked and played when the world was young and I had been younger. When the itch became too great to bear, my bag would be shouldered and off I would go, back to where it had all begun, in an attempt to recall the joys of that youth.

We live in a rapidly changing world, and the Africa that I knew has probably changed more quickly and more radically than most other lands. Whether she has changed for the better or for the worse is perhaps not for we old-timers to judge. We are dinosaurs and the nights are growing chilly. But I am glad that I knew the rainforests of Africa at their majestic best. The trees are mostly gone now and those that remain will never again be as tall and as spectacular as they were when I knew them. Back then, too, the song of the pepperbird was at its sweetest and the call of the secretive touraco in the forest clearing at its most haunting. The blue of the heavens was of such pristine delicacy that it could only have been devised by angels, and the long-legged jacana padding daintily over the lily pads on an inland waterway in the cool of the harmattan, evoked a vista of such ethereal beauty and tranquillity that your heart would break with nostalgia ever afterwards just to think about it.

Take this as gospel, for I know what I am talking about. I am one of *them*. I am a bushman and proud of it. We form a very exclusive clique, and we become more and more exclusive with the passing of each year.

1

Canoes Along the Gulf of Guinea

Youth is a time for dreaming. I suppose that, at one time or another, most of us have entertained our secret dreams of travelling to exotic lands and mingling on intimate terms with those icons who have captured our youthful hearts and imaginations in their own unique ways. The dreams, of course, were always of the fantastic, for what is the point in dreaming of the mundane? For an alarmingly high proportion of the female population of my own springtime years, the venue of such dreams was invariably Hollywood, where the film star Clark Gable was universally acknowledged to be the ultimate in sexual gratification. (An admiration not always shared, it transpired, by those leading ladies forced by satanic film directors to engage in passionate embrace with Mr Gable at crack of dawn: they found the screen idol's idiosyncrasy of soaking his false teeth overnight in a tumblerful of raw Kentucky bourbon a trifle hard to cope with so soon after their early morning kippers and poached eggs.) As for the lads, in their fantasies they were either shooting up outlaws with Hopalong Cassidy and his ilk or emulating the adventures of a variety of heroes in such weekly papers as the *Hotspur* and the *Rover*.

Whatever the fantasy, though, most of us were aware that it would remain just that – sheer, harmless fantasy. The girl who entertained dreams of torrid clinches with Gable would probably end up with some fairground attendant from Grimsby who could ill afford to sterilize his dentures in conventional cleansing agents, let alone expensive American bourbon, and the boy who hunted bandits around Wyoming in his imagination would eventually find himself, more often than not, driving a tractor full of manure around some God-forsaken croft on the Ayrshire moors, or wherever. My brother, whose dream was to ride the range with Dale Evans, wife of movie cowboy Roy Rogers, was never to meet her; he became a garage mechanic in a village in Wigtownshire, and a very good one at that. That just about says it all, really. When the dreamer takes his or her first tentative step into the big, bad world, the dreams of youth soon have to take second place to the harsh necessity of having to earn a living.

Like my brother, the focus of many of my youthful dreams was a lady. It was not, however, her looks that inter-ested me any more, I imagine, than they interested too many males of her era. Indeed, if this lady ever experienced lust for man in her short life, it remained a well-kept secret. She was tall and scraggy, of thin-faced, rather waspish features, and, although brought up in the sheltered refinery of Victorian London society, she had a vocabulary that would have blistered the paint on a Clyde-built tanker. She could handle a dugout canoe as well as any African, and Kipling wrote that he had never met anyone quite like her.

Her name was Mary Kingsley.

This indomitable lady travelled to West Africa during the last years of the nineteenth century. Her excuse for being there was that she was collecting insects, reptiles and small fishes for the British Museum, but escapism might have been closer to the truth – her overwhelming urge to flee from all the petty restrictions placed upon women in those days. She chose the forbidding swamps of the 'White Man's Grave' as her highway to the sort of freedom she craved.

Astonishingly, unsuited in the eyes of the casual observer though she might have seemed to life in such dire conditions, she took to it instantly, even though most of her time there was spent in the company of half-naked savages. As she had, initially, no one sponsoring her trip, she had to find money somehow to pay her way, and this she found by trading tobacco, fish hooks and fishing line for bars of wild rubber, the standard currency of the day.

Despite her rather severe appearance, she was a lady of considerable humour. One had to be to survive for long out there. On a visit to a tiny island in the Gulf of Guinea she was much taken by the beauty of the girls she met there. 'What a boon they would be to shipwrecked sailors,' she wrote. She was also a lady of not inconsiderable courage: 'I had a frill of them around my neck like an astrakhan collar,' she wrote of the time she emerged from a deep swamp covered in leeches.

A truly remarkable woman. It is said that as she lay dying of typhoid in South Africa in 1900 at the age of thirty-eight while nursing Boer prisoners of war, she asked that she be buried at sea in the hope that some part of her would drift northward towards her beloved forests and swamps of West Africa.

In all honesty, I cannot claim that it was solely through reading accounts of Miss Kingsley's travels that I ended up in the African rainforests myself some fifty years later. Even when at primary school, years before I had heard of the celebrated traveller, I remember daydreaming about going one day to roam the Dark Continent. But I am sure that, after I discovered them, her writings acted as a necessary spur. Perhaps, too, as with her, there was a certain degree of non-conformity in my makeup that helped. One didn't necessarily have to be a bit of a crank to want to go to such an outlandish place, but you probably had to have more than your fair share of eccentricity to wish to spend a large chunk of your life there. She spent five long years in this febrile land, at a time when medicaments were virtually non-existent and communication with the outside world impossible.

In considerably more favourable circumstances, I lived for something like thirty years as a forester in the rainforests of Africa, much of it spent either on water or in close proximity to it.

Fish and water go together, and quite often the warmer the water the stranger the creatures that inhabit it. The waters of the Gulf of Guinea abound with grouper and barracuda, both of which are well known to fishers of tropical seas. In their quite different ways they are magnificent fighters on the end of a line, and I have found both to make excellent fare. Hammerhead and tiger sharks also infest those waters, their fins clearly visible as they cruise up and down just beyond the shelf of the reef. They could be a horrible nuisance to the net fishers with their activities, charging repeatedly through the nets like torpedoes as though it were some kind of a game to them, but on the many occasions on which small ones got themselves inextricably entangled and were hauled up in one piece they, too, were eaten with enthusiasm by the men who paddled the long and gaily painted Fanti canoes. Occasionally turtles, mostly of the leatherback, the green and the hawksbill variety, would be caught up in the nets. The leatherback and the green turtles were not much more popular than the sharks with the fishermen, for they could make just as great a hash of the nets and there was generally much less profit to be made from them in the local markets for their flesh was not held in high esteem. Indeed, on the few occasions on which I ever tried turtle meat I found it to be tough and rubbery and not very pleasant-tasting. The hawksbill turtle was a more welcome catch: it was much smaller than the others, made less of a mess of the nets, and was reputed to be much better eating. In addition, there was a lot more money to be made from it, for it was the source of the much prized tortoiseshell jewellery.

Not all marine life in this part of the world had to grow to such sizes to be noticed. The seas around Africa were alive with even more spectacular sights, fishes that never amounted to more than a few centimetres in length: gobies, surgeonfishes, butterflyfishes, leaf-fishes and the like, fishes patterned in all the colours of the rainbow. They were eaten with avidity, for the coastal African is no sentimentalist where hunger and beauty are in conflict. I have watched as children waded through shallow tidal pools, scooping up those tiny, glowingly beautiful fishes by the bucketful, fishes that would have gladdened the heart of any aquarist had he had them in his collection, but that I knew for sure would have had their glorious colours boiled out of them by the time I next saw them on my plate later that night.

The French have a way with words. Their vocabulary is both expressive and romantic. To them the sea is feminine, and that is how I have always seen the sea. She is as capricious as she is beautiful, and she is never less than fascinating.

I have always been drawn to the sea, and particularly so in the tropics. In northern climes, when Atlantic gales whip her to a frenzy, she can be as savage as anywhere else in the world, but in those colder regions, even at the height of her fury, you know that the day will soon come when her temper will evaporate and she will decide that enough is enough. And one morning you will find that she has done just that. You sit on a cliff-top gazing out over an expanse of liquid glass of the most subtle and harmonious hues, with the kiss of the sun on dancing little waves at the mouth of the river that enters her the only visible indication that she is still a vibrant, living entity, a sea now at peace with herself where yesterday there was only seething turmoil, and you will wonder what all the fuss was about before.

But in Africa the sea is never still. She never sleeps. Day and night, the rollers come roaring in with relentless power. The noise never ceases, and it is always in the same sequence: the long, sad sough as she gathers her skirts for the charge . . . the rollicking, surging gallop that gets louder and louder and louder as the endless line of the great breaker gets nearer and nearer and nearer, a massive, moving wall of water crested by foam of the purest white . . . an infinitesimal pause in the charge as the breaker seems to hang, curving, over the shore, like some monstrous bird of prey hovering over its victim . . . then the pounce and the thunderous wallop as it disintegrates in a swirling confusion of spume, a wallop that shakes the ground around you even when you are well away from the point of impact.

Moonlit nights by a tropic sea are particularly magical, especially when one is on one's own. I realize that I may well be in a minority when asserting that, in order to appreciate fully the magnificence of such an environment, it would be better if you left the current love of your life behind. Instead take with you a flask of whichever medicinal warming fluid suits your taste, for even in tropical Africa there are certain times of the year when nights can be chilly. Your vigil will not be wasted. You will witness before you sights of such beauty and majesty as you are unlikely ever to see on your travels again: flickering rivulets of phosphorescence rippling and dancing over the surface of the dark, velvet waters like showers of stardust, creating a never-ending kaleidoscope of colour and never in the same place or following the same pattern. It is the aquatic equivalent of the Northern Lights. Along with the aurora borealis itself when seen from the edge of the ice floes, it ranks with me as being among the more spectacular of nature's showpieces.

I was witness to another phenomenon on a lonely West African beach during the course of one long night of brilliant moonlight. With the arrival of each thunderous breaker thousands of little red crabs were deposited on to the shore, only to instantly scamper back after the receding waters. It was a truly remarkable sight. In the brief hiatus between breakers the beach appeared empty of life, and the next moment it would be a seething mass of crabs. Curious-looking creatures they were too, for they seemed to be almost entirely composed of claws and long skinny legs, and their eyes were fiery orbs in the fulgent moonlight. Like the sea that carried them back and forth, they were never still. As each breaker towered over the shoreline I would quickly cast my eye along the wall of water as far as I could see, watching as its living red cargo cascaded upon the sand, only to pick themselves up immediately, scamper after the retreating waters and disappear once more into their shallows. With the next breaker, back they would tumble in shambolic disarray along the length of the beach, to scurry back into the sea again.

For hour after hour I watched them that night, and for hour upon hour the process was repeated. It seemed never-ending. What were they doing? I wondered. What was the purpose of this ceaseless activity? Was it some kind of a game? A sort of crustacean surfing competition without the surfboard? I am no expert on matters crustacean, but I guessed them to be some species of fiddler crab, common in many parts of the Tropics. However, I have since read that fiddlers are not normally renowned for their fondness for water, spending most of their time on land and diving down into their deep burrows when the tide comes in, remaining there, sustained by pockets of trapped air, until the tide goes out again. But maybe they were some other, related, species of crab? Or was this activity some kind of a mating frenzy? It is a mystery that remains with me.

Another crab to be found in considerable quantity on some of those tropic beaches was the aptly named ghost crab. This strange creature had the most perfect camouflage. It was of an almost transparent dun hue above and a very pale grey beneath, giving one the eerie feeling as it flitted over the sand that it had neither form nor substance. When predatory gulls cruised overhead it simply spread out its long legs and flattened itself, merging so well with the sand as to become virtually invisible. It could run like a streak, too, being by far the fastest-moving crab I have ever seen in my life. A large and lanky dog of low intellect that I had for a time and occasionally took to the beach with me drove himself to distraction trying – in vain – to catch one of them. I think what finally unhinged him was the fact that not only could this freak among shore life shoot off from a standing start at speeds that would have done justice to any whippet, but it did so in a *sideways* direction.

There is only so much a sensitive hound can take without finally cracking up.

The lagoons adjoining the West African coastline were also favourite places of mine. I have lived by them, all too briefly, from time to time. They were so open, and they were such cheerful places after the perpetual gloom of the rain-forests. On the lagoon the sun was with you all day long. There were no shadows, and there was none of the enervating mugginess of the high forest interior. Cooling winds, unrestricted by trees, blew in briskly over the low, narrow barrier of sand that separated the lagoon from the sea, ruffling one's hair and the surface of the water, making the little dark canoes of the fishermen bob and dance on the silver wavelets. Here and there, as you paddled leisurely along, great swards of close-cropped grass would be seen sweeping up the bank from the edge of the lagoon towards the home of some old colonial or other, the house barely visible behind a screen of bougainvillea. Colonials and missionaries always chose the most favourable locations for their dwellings, wherever they might benefit from whatever evening breezes happened their way.

More rarely, one might come upon the ruins of some ancient fortification, usually close to the lagoon shore and

half buried in scrub, a crumbling reminder of a past era
when those colourful adventurers the Portuguese braved
the killing fevers and the even more terrifying fears of the
mythical monsters reputed to abound in this inhospitable
land. They came to seek gold and diamonds, wild rubber
and ivory, and – inevitably – slaves. Many of them were destined to die before they even got properly started on the
long journey back to the overseas markets; while lagoon
waters were always placid, the same could not be said of the
sea where their ships had to lie at anchor beyond the reef
pending the return of their crews with the results of their
bartering inland. Even such wonderful seamen as the
Portuguese could come unstuck while trying in their heavily laden canoes to ride the mountainous breakers to reach
their ships. The toll in life was high. Slaves from upcountry
were rarely swimmers, and while their captors often were,
the local hammerheads were not in the slightest racist when
it came to a banquet of human flesh. Portuguese sailors or
African slaves, they all tasted much the same to those ferocious predators.

Coconut palms lined the lagoon shores, their lime-
green fronds swishing and crackling in the strong breezes,
while bossy black-and-yellow weaver birds, quarrelling
incessantly, tore long strips from the fronds to weave their
incredible nests. Occasionally small groups of laughing girls,
brown of body and teeth shining the whitest of white in the
sun, would be seen bathing at the water's edge. As you
drifted slowly past in your canoe they would stand in unself-
conscious nudity to wave and call greetings to you, the more
frisky among them signalling vigorously for you to come
over and join them.

The shallow, brackish waters of most of those lagoons

were full of very large prawns, ideal for the making of seafood dishes, and the small but delectable African black soles were quite common too. All one required in order to catch an abundance of sole-fish and prawns was an hour of your time, a boat with an outboard engine, and a home-made trawl to tow behind it, a facility made available to me once upon a time when I lived for a short period by the lovely Epe Lagoon in Nigeria.

If lagoons were among my more favourite places on the Coast, swamps were not. But, as with my heroine Mary Kingsley, the swamps and inland waterways were where I had to spend much of my time. Rivers, creeks and quag-mires had to be traversed when working in areas of lowland forest, and after a week or two floundering through those places you sometimes wondered whether your clothes would ever dry out and if your body would ever smell like that of a decent human being again. Wading through the average rainforest swamp was like wading waist-deep through warm farmyard slurry while being slowly but surely asphyxiated by its foetid, gaseous emissions. Insects of all denominations were in clouds, and each and every one of them fed on blood, preferably human. The fishermen who spent their lives by those waters must have had hides like buffaloes, but even so chronic malaria was rife and the inci-dence of infant mortality astronomically high.

While staying for a time in a fishing village among the creeks I was told a tale about a girl who got lost in a vast swamp while she was out gathering crabs. Seeking a place in which to stay the night, she came upon a tiny islet on which lived a solitary old fisherman. Mosquitoes were particularly savage in that area, so the old man suggested that she share his mosquito net for the night. Being a virtuous girl and fearing the old man's intentions more than she feared those of the mosquitoes, she declined his offer and slept on the ground outside his hut. The following day she caught cerebral malaria and died within hours of reaching home.

A year later her sister happened upon the same islet while she was out fishing in her canoe. Dusk was upon her, and the old man made the same offer to her as he had made to her sister. She – sensible girl that she was – accepted with alacrity. She left the fisherman a few days later with not a single mosquito bite on her whole body, while the broad smile with which she greeted all she met as she paddled her way slowly homeward gave notice that her nights spent with the old man under his mosquito net had not been such a disagreeable experience after all.

Motto: What good are high moral standards if they are going to be the death of you?

In the waterways close to the Gulf of Guinea the people lived almost entirely on fish: fish boiled, fish baked, fish fried, fish stewed, fish smoked, and fish in various stages of decay. Not surprisingly, they and their dwellings stank to high heaven of fish. It was only when I ceased to notice the smell that I realized that I, too, must be stinking of fish. While mostly it was catfish they caught, occasionally they would succeed in trapping one of the rare little dwarf crocodiles, shy and inoffensive creatures rarely surpassing five feet in length. These were considered a delicacy, their flesh being rather like chicken both in appearance and in taste.

Dugout canoes were the usual mode of transport on the coastal waterways. Very occasionally, where the water was deep enough and the paying passenger trade steady enough to warrant the expense, the owner might have an outboard motor fitted to the stern. But it was a rare occurrence. The average owner of a dugout canoe was generally too poor to be able to afford such a refinement. In any case, he was often a fisherman or a hunter, and silence was of the essence in his occupation. Engines also needed not only access to fuel but the wherewithal to buy the fuel on a regular basis, and they needed someone with sufficient mechanical knowledge to operate the machine and effect repairs to it when necessary. In addition, the narrower channels were shallow and invariably clogged with weeds, constantly fouling up the propeller shaft. In such conditions, paddle canoes were a decided advantage. Indeed, whatever the conditions, I much preferred the latter. When the soft swish of the paddle thrusting through the water was the only sound to offend the ears one could relax and enjoy the tranquil sounds of the life of the water and the surrounding forest. When amidst primitive natural beauty, in whichever part of the world I have happened to find myself, the harsh racketing of an engine has never failed to set my teeth on edge.

The lengths and types of canoes varied considerably. Different tribes had different needs, and they had their own ideas as to lengths, shapes and species of tree best suited to their needs. It often depended, too, upon the prevalence of a particular tree species in a particular area as to what type of tree would be used. People living alongside small inland waterways far from the sea tended to favour small canoes of light and perishable timber. They were horribly unstable and bobbed about like corks in even the slightest ripples. They soon rotted away, too, for the African of the interior had no knowledge of, or access to, wood preservatives. But the advantage was that they were easily replaced, for the trees from which they were made, having timber as soft as cheese, could be rapidly converted into canoes. As one progressed further and further south and into the slow-moving, deep waterways nearer the sea, where the inhabitants relied more on fishing and less on actual hunting, the canoes got longer and longer and heavier and heavier, for they were generally made of such dour, imperishable species as ekki, the ironwood of the Coast. These took a very long time to make, for, even in a freshly felled, green state, the wood was very hard indeed, and since adzes and axes were the only tools available, the work involved in converting a long, thick tree trunk in the hot humidity of a small forest clearing was onerous in the extreme. But these canoe makers were accomplished craftsmen. The finished item was always a work of art that would be in service for many years to come.

The rivers, creeks, lagoons and swamps were the commercial arteries of the lands bordering the Gulf of Guinea. The dugout canoe was taxi, private car, passenger coach and goods lorry all combined. A person could travel, quite undetected, for many miles on those waters from one point to another should he or she so desire, or should it have been deemed necessary to do so for reasons legal or illegal. And these canoes could carry incredible loads. I once witnessed a canoe about twelve feet in length and not much more than two feet wide at the centre loaded down to such an extent that the water was literally lipping the gunwales. It contained a man and his wife, six trussed fowls, two children, three goats and several dozen five-gallon tin containers full of can-can (a highly toxic distillation from sugar-cane) piled row upon row on top of each other. On top was tied a canvas deckchair and, resting on top of that, a folded black umbrella. The man was singing happily as he steadfastly paddled forward. The lagoon on which he was travelling

was as placid as lagoon waters usually were, but God knows
how he would manage when he reached the choppier waters
at the far end where the lagoon met the river mouth.

On another occasion I was heading in a Land Rover
towards a wide river that boasted a ferry capable of carrying
a motor vehicle. I had never been in this area before, but my
confidence in West African ferries was not high, having
experienced them in the past. I was not disappointed: the
ferry turned out to be a frightening contraption consisting of
four long and venerable canoes, each one crewed by four
villainous-looking thugs. The canoes supported a very
flimsy framework of long saplings lashed together with
lengths of liane, and a decking of planks had been nailed on
top of the poles to form a sort of raft. I found it hard to
believe that vehicles were actually able to cross on this awful
thing, but my driver assured me that he had used it several
times in the recent past. Some loose planks that had been
stacked on the ferry were placed between the bank and the
deck while the ferrymen, straining on ropes from the bank,
held it more or less steady and in place in the water. Over
this crazy ramp my driver cautiously guided his vehicle.
With the weight of the vehicle the raft slowly settled down
in the water to a depth of about a foot, while the crew frantically fixed ropes between vehicle and ferry to prevent the
unthinkable from happening. While all this was going on a
couple of Fulani herdsmen had appeared with half a dozen
of their long-horned, humpbacked cattle, waiting for their
turn to cross. Politely declining an invitation to cross along
with my driver and his vehicle and opting instead to cross
with the cows, I sat on the bank chatting to the two cattlemen while I watched with a certain morbid interest the
precarious trip over the river. Land Rover and driver made

it, of course, for the paddlers obviously knew what they were doing, but it looked nonetheless hazardous to me.

I crossed with the Fulanis and their cattle. I was still not very happy about the whole business although the cattle stood still and, with its very much lighter load, the ferry seemed marginally safer. At the other side Ebenezer, my driver, was openly resentful: 'Why massa no de come on ferry with me? Massa fear to cross with his driver, but he no de fear to cross with cow?'

'Because,' I replied truthfully, 'I no de savvy swim. I been sure you would end up in river, and I no agree for die yet.'

'But you no de fear drown for river if ferry sink with cow?' he persisted pointedly.

'Yes, I fear,' I said patiently. 'But cow de savvy swim, and Fulani cow get long horn. If I dey for water and I catch hold of horn, cow go carry me to bank. Ebenezer no get horns, and de only horn Land Rover get, na wahallah (noise) horn. And besides, Land Rover no de savvy swim, either.'

The logic of my reply mollified him somewhat. But I never made that crossing again, and I would have travelled many a long mile to ensure that I never had to do so.

Not all Africans of the coastal regions were true fishermen. Those tribes who were universally recognized as being true fishing people were, in fact, comparatively few in number and they guarded their rights to fish their individual tribal waters jealously. The Krous of the Ivory Coast and Liberia, the Fantis of Ghana and the Ijaws of Nigeria were three of the larger and better known of the purely fishing tribes scattered along the coastline of the Gulf. Their children could handle canoes from a very early age, and a frequent sight on any of the narrow little waterpaths that linked the swamps and creeks and rivers of the deltas would be that of some stark naked little boy, six or seven years of age at most, poling a long canoe with all the confidence of a man as he balanced on the little platform at its stern.

White people were almost never encountered in dugout canoes. On the very rare occasion on which I did meet one, he was almost always a missionary. Being of no particular religious persuasion myself, I was, like Mary Kingsley, sometimes a bit sceptical about their objectives, but I had to acknowledge the fact that they were supremely dedicated people and generally well liked by the forest Africans. They were also, with few exceptions, characters in their own right. One such was the Reverend Father Joseph Murnaghan.

I had known Joe for some years and we were good friends. He was called the 'Fisherman's Priest' by the local swamp tribes, and not without reason, for his beat covered some of the more waterlogged territory in all of West Africa.

He was a keen angler himself, and on those occasions on which I was able to spend a weekend at his little mission among the creeks, we would often go fishing for catfish and perch. We were out in his canoe one evening, he paddling while I trolled a cichlid fixed to a spoon behind the boat. I had a strike, and by the heavy, sustained downward pull on the rod I assumed it to be a catfish. I manoeuvred my catch to the stern of the boat and Joe reached down to lift it out of the water by the gills.

'Shit!' he exclaimed violently, recoiling so sharply that he almost turned the canoe over. He was doubled up in obvious pain and shock. 'What the bloody hell was that?'

Puzzled and alarmed, I cautiously reeled the fish in to

my end of the canoe. 'Careful!' warned Joe. 'Don't touch it – the bugger's wired to the mains!'

I peered down at my trophy. Nothing could have persuaded me to touch it when I saw what it was. The good Father's description, colourful though it may have been, was not all that far from the truth. His assailant, to be precise, was an electric catfish of around two feet in length. I had seen this fish only once before in my life and, like all creatures in Africa with unique abilities, much highly exaggerated folklore was attached to it. It was a curious-looking creature, fat and stubby and rather harmless in appearance, but I knew it to be quite capable of administering a hefty shock of up to a hundred volts from organs situated just under its skin all along the length of its body. It was a ferocious predator and quite fearless. With a kick like that, it had every reason to be.

And perhaps a priest had every right to be mortified at being zapped like that by a fish of all things. The fish, after all, was one of the most venerated of all the ancient Christian symbols.

But it was with a new respect that I regarded the Reverend Father Joseph Murnaghan thereafter. With such an admirable command of Anglo-Saxon expletives, even the heretical Miss Kingsley might have revised her lowly opinion of missionaries had she ever had the opportunity of meeting him.

2

The Man Who Liked Flowers

Strathoni was by no means the first house I occupied in West Africa, but it was certainly the most memorable. I was on my first tour of the Coast and, after being shoved around from pillar to post for some considerable time while those responsible for my being in Africa in the first place wondered what on earth to do with me, I found myself in this part of Nigeria's Ondo Province. It was love at first sight.

I was never to discover the identity of the homesick expatriate who gave the house and its surroundings such a resoundingly Scottish name. It was perhaps not quite so inappropriate as it might first have seemed to the casual visitor, though, for at the height of the dry season the Oni River, on whose bank the house stood, eddied and swirled and tumbled over and around mossy rocks and smooth boulders and gravel beds, its waters as sparkling clear as those of any Scottish Highland river.

   Whichever long-forgotten engineer had been responsible for selecting the site must have had an eye for the aesthetic as well as for the future prosperity of the logging company who were paying him. Trees must have completely surrounded the site while the house was under construction, for this area, though well to the north of the watery Delta regions, was still within the rainforest zone. By the time of my arrival, however, much had changed. The great forests to the north-east of the river had gone, flattened en masse by the pernicious timber people, to be replaced by endless tracts of cocoa and coffee interspersed with patches of yam and cassava. Here and there, too, one would encounter little plots of tobacco, the pretty pink flowers exuding a sweet fragrance as one walked through the large, fleshy, dark-green leaves while the early morning dew still hung heavy upon them. On the other side of the river, and for fifty miles and more to the south, west and east, the vast forests were still untouched and were liable to remain so for the forseeable future, for the existing colonial authorities had declared that part of the country a forest reserve.

   The house was situated on the northern bank of the river. It was a neat bungalow of cement-faced mud block, the walls whitewashed a pristine white each dry season. The roof consisted of grey corrugated-asbestos sheeting. The frontage faced the river and a wooden verandah ran along its length. It was not a large house by colonial standards but it was adequate enough for a childless couple or – as was more often the case – single people like myself. Behind its French windows there was a small living room, a reasonably spacious main bedroom and a tiny spare bedroom. To the rear of the house and separate from it was the kitchen, a sturdy edifice of the usual mud block, and well to the rear of that a little corrugated-iron shed that housed a small generator for the electricity supply, a feature not at all prevalent among houses as far up-country as Strathoni. A great ceiling fan in the centre of the living room shunted the hot air around during the more oppressively humid nights of the rain season.

The furniture was more functional than elegant. Half a dozen armchairs of the darkest mahogany, so solid in appearance that they looked as timeless and as sturdy as the trees from which they had been manufactured, were scattered around the living room. Someone – possibly the previous occupant's wife – had made an effort to soften their severity by covering their big square cushions with heavy, jet-black brocade trimmed with gold lace. Chairs of the same dark timber encircled the African walnut dining room table set in a little alcove off the living room, and the mahogany plank floor glowed with a lustrous patina from repeated polishing.

The compound was spacious, spreading downhill from the house all the way to the river fully sixty yards away. Harsh African grass covered most of it, but there were plenty of small trees and shrubs too. Yellow-and-pink-flowering cassias, hibiscus with scarlet and white flowers, and frangipani, so weirdly branched as to resemble escapees from the Mojave Desert but with waxy, cream-coloured flowers that emitted one of the headiest perfumes in all of Africa, were dotted all over the place, while a large, showy, purple bougainvillea draped itself with untidy abandon over the far corner of the verandah rail. On the edge of the compound a tall kapok tree released its cottony seeds in clouds during the hot, dry months of December and January, giving one the impression of having been caught in a snowstorm when this astonishing spectacle was encountered for the first time, and during those same months a fifty-yard stretch of the bank of the river would suddenly be highlighted with a delicate orange glow when a thick border of harmattan lilies burst into glorious inflorescence.

The whole of the western side of the compound was taken up by a large orchard of avocado, grapefruit, orange and lime trees, and behind were large plots of different varieties of bananas and pineapples. The Strathoni fruit were reckoned to be of superior quality and were therefore much sought after by visiting expatriates. Few left the house without at least a crate full of fruit in the backs of their vehicles. Monkeys liked them too, and troupes of them would cross the river to lay periodic waste to them. However, so copious was the yield of fruit – most of the time a thick carpet of rotting avocados, grapefruit and oranges covered the ground under the trees – that their depredations made little impact.

Hereabouts the Oni River was about fifty yards wide, and at a point below the house and a short distance to the east it was bridged by huge ironwood beams set on formidable piers of stone and concrete. Occasionally, during particularly severe rain seasons, these beams, along with their attached decking planks, would be washed away in the roaring torrent, leaving whoever was occupant of the house well and truly cut off from the outside world until the floods had subsided and the bridge could be repaired.

Not that it made much difference, for the road that it served was generally quite impassable at times like those in any case. It was not so much a road as a track, one that began at Agbaje Waterside, a logging station far to the south among the Okitipupa creeks. Forging almost due north, it cut through scrub and patches of farmland for a few miles before bisecting the main Benin to Lagos road – in itself, little more than a rutted track for much of its length – then surging deeper and deeper through the darkness of the high forests towards the Oni River. In the dry season this was a well-maintained road, for loggers operated in the forests far to the north of the Oni and it was in their own interest to keep it in good condition for the huge trucks that daily thundered along with their huge cargoes of massive logs. But in the months of the rains when the logging company had shut its bush operations down to concentrate on servicing vehicles at the Agbaje headquarters, sections of the road would degenerate into a quagmire. There was nothing for the expatriate living upcountry to do but to shrug his shoulders and await the arrival of the dry season once more.

It never bothered me a great deal whether the road was open or not. It was true that during the dry season things were more comfortable from the domestic point of view. Expatriate wives at headquarters would make periodic trips over the long, long trail to Lagos to purchase frozen foods and such luxuries from the supermarkets there, and in due course whoever happened to be resident at Strathoni would receive his share. It made a pleasant change, I suppose, from bush meat, but I personally cared little whether I found myself dining on leg of New Zealand lamb or leg of African goat.

Employee numbers around the Strathoni compound were kept to the bare minimum. In the little office across the road from the house I had David, a tubercular Ibo clerk, and the harsh barking of his cough made one's lungs ache just to listen to it. He was a good clerk and a most obliging fellow, but his consumptive splatters were on every document he handed to me. I was relieved when, soon after I arrived in the area, he left for his homeland to consult his favourite witchdoctor about it. The cure, I learned some time later, was as instant as it was effective: twelve hours after swallowing the potion administered to him, he died.

My major domo was Peter, a lovely lad with a bad stammer who was to remain in my employ for fifteen years. He was an intelligent chap and I taught him the basics of writing, although I had neither the time nor the inclination to introduce him to the mysteries of grammar and spelling. He was very proud of his new-found literacy, and when news would arrive that some expatriate wife was heading for the city to do some shopping for the area, Peter would present his list to me for vetting. His spelling of words, written exactly as he pronounced them himself, could exercise the mind until one got used to it. Baking soda appeared as 'bekkin soddink', tinned milk as 'millik', pork sausage as 'poksossishish', and haricot beans as 'harlotica beens'. A curious item written as 'slivverlif pitshis' puzzled me initially until I found out that it referred to a brand of canned peaches known as Silver Leaf.

Peter's duties could never have been termed onerous. I think, while looking back on that period of my life now, that he probably had one of the most pleasant jobs in all of Africa. Personal 'boys' did not always have it easy, particularly in a household with a colonial wife around. Relations between the cook-steward and the 'madame' could sometimes be fragile, for the lady would be able to find dust where bachelors such as I neither saw nor cared. I doubt if I gave Peter more than a dozen instructions in all the years we were together. I never had to: he was supremely efficient at his job. He knew exactly what I wanted around the house and he went about his duties without fuss. He cooked my food not only to my own satisfaction but to that of the few visitors I ever entertained. He washed and ironed my clothes daily, he polished the floor each morning, and he kept the house tidy. He woke me up with a pot of tea at my bedside each morning, he prepared my bath every evening when I came home from work, he laid out the clothes he thought I should wear, and he brought me my nightcap after dinner. He was a black Jeeves, the complete gentleman's gentleman, and to the day we parted we had an enormous respect for each other.

On the very odd occasion when he found himself saddled with an irksome and time-consuming task, Peter would draft in Paraffin Oil to help him. Paraffin Oil was a relative, perhaps, even, a son, though I never found out for sure, and he was about six years of age. Sometimes hunters would bring in baby animals such as antelopes and hyraces and so on, orphaned when they had shot the mothers for food. For a few pennies each week Paraffin Oil would be employed to feed the tiny creatures and, as he obviously had an astonishing affinity with wild things, some even survived. In between feeding chores he would go down to the river with Peter to help wash my clothes. One of my more entertaining memories is of watching him walk down the hill, a small pan of clothes balanced on his head and a bushbaby sitting on his shoulder. The little thing's great luminous eyes were closed contentedly as it clutched the boy's ear with its hands while it suckled away at the lobe. Peter informed me later that Paraffin Oil had smeared the lobe of his ear with honey to keep the little fellow occupied while he helped with the washing.

The compound was very large indeed. Large compounds needed constant attention, otherwise they soon returned to their original wild state. Grass cutting was a major factor in preventing this from happening, and 'garden boys' were employed for this most boring of chores. The term 'garden boy' was something of a euphemism, for the 'boy' was generally a middle-aged man, and he was almost never a gardener in the accepted sense of the word. Grass cutting was usually his only skill, and he would consider it an imposition to be given a spade and told to dig a hole. But grass cutting full-time was a back-breaking job, and even the most unimaginative of employees found it tedious. The moment the boss had departed it was down tools and off to find a cool, shady spot to while away the time in pleasant dreams. I could not blame them: swishing away for hour after hour under the blazing African sun with their implements must have been mind-numbing in the extreme.

Gardeners did not generally have a long shelf life. Those at Strathoni were no exception. They came and they went with such rapidity that I do not recall any of their faces as I write this. They were just slashers of grass, and when you have seen one slasher of grass you have seen them all. But there was one garden boy who will remain forever green in my memory. We became friends, and I remember him now as the Flower Man.

He was skeletal of body and wizened of mien. His skin was that greyish black hue that one tended to find with members of certain tribes, as though the natural skin colour was permanently coated with a layer of fine dust. In appearance, he was the most insignificant of men – if, in fact, you were to notice him at all, he would have made as little impact upon you as the green migrant butterflies that drifted over the land every harmattan on their way north to the savannahs of the Fulani. His expression was one of permanent gloom, and in the whole year he was with me I don't suppose I saw him smile more than a couple of times. He was always barefoot, and the only thing I ever saw him wearing was a tatty old piece of monkey skin around his scrawny loins.

I had initially hired him as a trace-cutter for my survey gang. He was a steady – if unenthusiastic – worker, but he was obviously a bit of a loner and ill at ease among the others. He had none of their infectious joie de vivre and, indeed, they would have nothing to do with him. This did not surprise me a lot, for they were Yorubas while he came from far to the east of the Niger. It was not that one could say that there was any overt hostility, but tribal hatreds were ever ready to erupt at the slightest excuse and, when even the foreman in charge began to grumble, I decided to remove him and set him to work cutting grass in the Strathoni compound.

He liked it there. He was on his own, and that suited him. His body gleamed with sweat in the noonday sun as his whippy, long-bladed slashing iron flailed back and forth over the grassy surface. Now and again bursts of staccato, high-pitched song would erupt from him, awful, tuneless emissions, but at least it was a change from the silent and unnatural acquiesance with which he had accepted the jibes and calculated insults of the others in the survey gang. When I returned from work each evening he would still be there, his day's toil over but politely waiting to ensure that there was nothing further I required from him before he went about his own business.

To my mild surprise, he took an interest in gardening, in growing things. Especially flowers. He loved colour, and he would bring all sorts of beautiful wild plants in from the forest across the river and attempt to grow them in the wet soil of the river bank. A few survived, but most died when suddenly exposed to sunlight after the gloom of the forest. He then hit on the idea of erecting a protective cover of palm leaves over them and his success rate improved dramatically. Encouraged, he began to plant in the shade of the orchard, and he even had a go at introducing orchids to the forks of some of the trees. Great was his pride when he even succeeded with two of them.

Flowers became a daily feature in the Strathoni house. It was something that I had never bothered with before, but now never a day passed without me returning from work to find vases in the house ablaze with colour from the variety of flowers that he had gathered earlier in the day and handed over to Peter for his attention.

The Flower Man had built himself a hut of poles and bark in a clearing half a mile downriver from my house. I never saw anyone near it, none of the gaggles of friends normally accumulated in short order by the highly gregarious bush African wherever he happened to find himself. 'I am a stranger in a strange land,' he would reply philosophically when I asked him why he had no woman to look after him.

He was not only literate but he was also highly intelligent, and I also found him to be of a deeply religious bent. I came across him sitting on a bench outside his hut one Sunday afternoon, reading a well-worn bible. 'Catholic school in Umuahia,' was his terse reply in response to my query. That was about as communicative as he ever became regarding his background. But then, he rarely spoke anyway unless spoken to first, and any response he made even then would generally be in the form of some quaintly appropriate biblical quotation.

I was soon to discover that he was both a good hunter

and a keen fisherman. He had every Saturday afternoon and Sunday off work, so much of his free time was spent in checking the fish traps that he had set in the wide, deep pool on the river to the west of my house. He had constructed a dugout canoe that he kept moored at the edge of the pool, and when he was not checking his traps he could often be seen out in the middle of the river handlining for catfish. But most nights invariably saw him setting off into the forest with his hunter's lamp strapped to his forehead and his ancient flintlock over his shoulder. Occasionally I would wonder idly to myself as to what ungodly hour he would return from those nocturnal expeditions, or whether, in fact, he spent what was left of the night sleeping out in the forest. But it was not a thought that bothered me a lot; the only thing that mattered to me was that he was always at work on time each morning, swinging his slasher with the same monotonous rhythm, accompanying his swings with the same monotonous chant.

The woods around us were alive with game and every pool on the river was full of fish of all kinds. I decided to make occasional use of his expertise to add some variety to my standard fare of tinned food and goat and scraggy African chickens. I broached the subject to him one evening as he was passing my house on his way to the forest:

'Every Sunday, bring me good bush meat. I want it to be fresh, and I want it to be *proper* meat. No bloody monkeys or hornbills or snakes. Just good meat like guinea-fowl and antelope. Na white-man chop. You understand?'

'Your servant heareth, Lord,' he quoted lugubriously.

'Also,' I continued, 'maybe sometimes, when I'm free, I'd like to go fishing with you, so check with me each Sunday before you go off to look at your fish traps.'

'I will be happy to have you with me any time you care,' he assured me gravely.

He smiled his rare, sad smile, shouldered his musket, and evanesced into the shadows of the tall trees behind the compound.

Sometimes as I sat on my verandah enjoying a cold beer in the cool of the evening I would see him passing by on his way to the forest or to his fish traps. Intriguingly, he would always stop to pick a flower from my compound – a yellow canna, a scarlet poinciana or one of the orange lilies from the river bank – to stick in his wiry black hair. 'Na my juju, massa,' he explained. 'Wear a flower when you go hunting or fishing, and you will never return empty-handed.'

Nor did he. He never failed to bring me something or other every Sunday morning on his return from the forest, whether it happened to be a brace of fine, fat guinea-fowl or a duiker or the tender back quarters of a waterbuck. Sometimes of a weekday morning he would have a large, black, gleaming catfish, cleaned and gutted, to present to my cook to prepare for my evening meal. Catfish were common around this part, and the fishtraps in the river would often yield one or two of these succulent fish.

Very occasionally, if I warned him in advance that I had friends coming for dinner on a particular weekend, he would bring me a special treat: a large, tender haunch of meat ready for roasting, skinned and neatly boned and wrapped in banana leaves. 'Na some kinda bush-pig,' he explained vaguely when I asked him once what it was, and I always rewarded him handsomely on those occasions.

For those roasts were well worth the money. They were absolutely delectable, and that was a period in my life when I could pride myself on the fact that the MacIntosh table had become something of a byword among certain expatriate homes. Gourmets who had an appreciation of good food licked their lips in anticipation for days beforehand when they heard that my employee's roast was to be on the menu.

He was also an expert with the cast-net. One of his regular haunts for this sort of fishing was the wide, shallow pool right at the foot of my compound. I would watch him from my verandah on Sunday evenings, marvelling at his dexterity in an art that I had never been able to master myself.

The cast-net was strictly for use in shallow water, and only of use in the catching of small fish (which were usually more prized by the bush African for his stews than the larger ones). The cast-net somewhat resembled a circular skirt, weighted with bits of scrap iron and stones around its fringe, and with a drawstring passing around its bottom edge and coming out through its narrow neck. It was thrown over the pool, fanning out in a perfect circle, the weights around its hem carrying it down. A pull of the string closed it into a bag-net, with everything under it trapped inside, and it would then be carefully hauled back to the bank.

It was by no means as easy as it looked. There was a definite art to the casting of the net, for a start, in the same way as there was an art to the way in which the South American gaucho threw his bolas. One slight error of judgement, one slight loss of concentration, and painful things could happen to the operator.

But not to my Flower Man. He was an expert. I can see him now as I write . . .

He has taken off his loinskin covering and placed it on the flat shelf of rock behind him. He stands stark naked on a large boulder by the water's edge, his back to me, his skinny frame gleaming dully in the sunlight. He bends down and lets his net trail in the water to make it supple, then he stands up and shakes it to make sure that there are no snarls in it to foul up his cast. He feels for the hem of the net, lifting one of the weights and taking it in his mouth. Then, with the drawstring in his left hand, he reaches out with his other hand to take in another bit of hem. He now has a hold of the net with his left hand, his mouth, and his right hand. Holding his left hand far outstretched behind him, he swings suddenly, hard but gracefully, with a horizontal arcing movement of his right hand, releasing – at exactly the correct moment – the ends held by his left hand and his teeth. The whirling net seems to hang momentarily in the air above the water with circumfluent elegance, like the 'umbrella' of a colossal jellyfish, before settling over the pool with barely a splash. He waits, perfectly still, allowing the net just enough time to sink evenly to the river bottom, then he pulls on the drawstring . . .

Crayfish were caught in abundance by this method, and the larger ones could be turned into excellent scampi, once I had taught my cook how to do it. But I liked the African way best, and, on the very odd occasion on which this strange man would invite me to dine with him in his spartan hut on the edge of the clearing, I would gladly accept. Oddly enough, meat was never on the menu on those occasions; he much preferred fish, he told me. In fact, the meal was always the same: a delicious stew of crayfish, peppers and okra, cassava or yam, and garnished with plenty of wild benniseed with a calabash of palm wine making the perfect accompaniment.

At times like those he would open up a bit more than was his wont. He could talk quite eloquently on subjects that were close to his heart. He was fascinating when talking about the ways of the wild, and his love for all the creatures of the forest shone through in our discussions and in his stories. Most of all, though, he was interested in biblical subjects. The story of the life of Christ intrigued him, and he would fire question after question at me, questions that made me more than a little uncomfortable, for it was patently obvious to me from the beginning that he knew far more about biblical matters than I did.

When I went out with him in his canoe, I would take with me a cheap spinning rod to troll or spin for perch and carp and tigerfish in the deep pools under the shade of the trees on the other side of the river. He showed no interest at all in this type of fishing, even going so far on one occasion as to reprove me gently for my delight when I landed a particularly fine tigerfish after a prolonged struggle. 'The creatures of the earth and the waters have been granted by God for men to use as and when they need them,' he said, 'but not for men to take pleasure in their humiliation and death.'

He was expert at the many African ways of catching fish, but it was never a sporting business with him. He caught just enough to satisfy his needs, with – sometimes – a bit over to sell in the Sunday market in the village up the road from Strathoni. Shallow waters where fish congregated at certain times of the day were favourite places to set his wicker traps. They were also preferred spots for the amphibious and highly lethal black forest cobra to prowl in search of fish and frogs. On one occasion when I was helping him check his traps in murky water only his sharp warning made me pull my hand away in time from a trap that contained a large and infuriated serpent.

He used a variety of plants for catching fish in those still waters, too. I remember that one was a vetch-like plant called, locally, 'igun'. When a branch of igun was placed in the water it had the effect of blinding and stupefying all the fish in the vicinity, and the fruits of certain large forest trees were used by him to much the same effect.

But he was, I think, happiest on his own, and I never went out with him except by invitation. I had work to do, so I never saw him during the day. Most of the time my only sight of him would be when I came home from work when the kapok tree was casting its long evening shadow over the compound, or when I would catch a glimpse of his figure disappearing into the forest, gun over his shoulder and the inevitable flower stuck in his hair. He was the quietest of people, and he caused me less trouble than just about any employee I ever had.

December came, and the chill harmattan haze settled in a grey blanket over Nigeria. Suddenly, he informed me that he had just received a message from his homeland to say that his father was dying. He had to leave immediately, he said, and it was unlikely that he would return. I was sorry to see him go. I wrote the obligatory reference for him, awarded him a handsome bonus for all his good work, and wished him well. He thanked me with his usual courtesy. 'Blessed is he that considereth the poor,' he quoted gravely. 'You have been as my father and my mother while I have been here.' Then he was gone.

I never saw him again.

We were sitting in an expatriate club not far from the Niger. My companion was staying overnight in town to clear up some odds and ends in connection with his recent murder

case before making his way back upcountry to his station. It
was still early evening, so we had this normally busy club to
ourselves.

I had met him only once before. He was one of the
most senior police officers in the country, and he had a very
tough reputation. During the past few months he had been
in charge of an undercover operation to stamp out the activities of the Leopard Society, a notorious cult linked to a
recent spate of murders and ritual cannibalism along the
Niger. Gunned down in the operation had been my Flower
Man.

In his tiny hut the police had found clear evidence to
prove that he had been very busy indeed since leaving my
employ, and that he had been a prominent local leader of
this branch of the cult for many years before that. The reference I had written for him on his departure, framed and
proudly displayed on the wall of his hut, had led the police
to me.

'One thing puzzles me,' mused the policeman. 'After we
had shot him and removed his leopard mask, we found
something stuck in his hair. A flower. And on the table in his
hut we found a bible. Open at the Book of St John.' His cold
policeman's eyes were suddenly drilling out through mine.
'Now what kind of a maniac would put flowers in his hair
and read the Bible before going out to murder someone, I
ask you?'

I looked down at my beer. Two fat, copulating flies had
tumbled into it and were thrashing around in the froth. I
fished them out with my forefinger and squashed them on
the coaster with my thumb. They made a scrunching sound,
like eggshells being broken. He glared at me in revulsion.
'Don't *do* that for Christ's sake, you gruesome bastard!' he

shuddered. I wondered idly at the psychology of a man who could be so obviously repelled by the killing of a couple of bluebottles, yet think nothing about the gunning down of a fellow human being in cold blood.

'But what on earth,' I enquired in the ensuing silence, 'was he doing so far from home and working as a common garden boy for me?'

He smiled, but it was a smile that was as bleak as a Siberian winter. 'On sabbatical, maybe,' he replied. Then he added with gallows humour: 'Or then again, maybe not.'

I thought about my Flower Man, with his biblical quotations and his succulent catfish and those delectable Sunday roasts.

Especially, those delectable Sunday roasts.

Suddenly, I didn't feel too good myself.

3

The Fishing Baboon

For a mercifully brief period of time, I did some work for a Lebanese timber exporting agency in West Africa. My work in the forest was, as always, pleasant enough; the boring times were when I had to return periodically to camp to deliver my reports. European accommodation on the Coast ranged from the quietly comfortable to the decidedly opulent, but for some reason Lebanese houses had a drabness about them that deadened the soul. They were spartan to an extreme. There were no pictures on the walls, no flowers in vases to add a bit of cheer and colour to the interior, no carpets on the floors, and the furniture would invariably consist of great, solid lumps of things that would not have looked out of place in a sanatorium for the criminally insane. Windows of crudely hewn latticework were reinforced with rusty iron bars, while the bathroom facilities were of the style, appearance and fragrance familiar to the undiscriminating habitué of the less pretentious fornicatoriums of downtown Beirut. Beds were starkly functional, rarely being blessed with mosquito netting. Conversation always seemed to be conducted in harsh, angry torrents of words and at the pitch of their voices. Laughter was rare, and few seemed interested in – or, indeed, to have much knowledge of – any subject unconnected with money and the acquisition thereof. 'We are the Jews of West Africa,' declared one of my Lebanese acquaintances once with unconscious irony.

The seaside town was only a few miles away, and it was always a relief to escape the dreariness of the Lebanese camp on the pretext of having to buy some supplies for my next trip to bush. Two internationally renowned shipping companies operated from there, one French and the other German, and I could always depend on a cold beer and some friendly chat with their expatriate staff any time I called. It was in the French compound that I first met the Monkey Woman.

She was standing under a mango tree, clad in blue shorts and a wet, very grubby white T-shirt bearing the logo 'Sock it to me, Daddy'. A large pan of soapy water containing a wire scrubbing brush was by her feet, and in her hand she held a hose from which she was directing a powerful jet of water at an ape shackled to the end of a long chain attached to the trunk of the tree. From its frantic, evasive bounds and its yells of wrath, I gathered that bathing was not an exercise that appealed to it very much.

I studied her. She was as scrawny as a maribou stork and just about as prepossessing. Although probably no more than twenty years of age, her face had a distinctly lived-in quality. She looked for all the world like a jet-black version of Popeye's Olive Oyl.

She glanced irritably at me. 'Hold this bloody monkey still for me while I give it a bath.'

'Certainly not!'

She laid down the hose and stared coldly at me. The ape stopped squalling and bared its fangs. They were long and sharp and ochre-coloured. Its eyes were shrewd and darting, the woman's steady and worldly-wise. 'Is it me or the monkey you're afraid of, white man?'

I looked at the creature's fangs again and spoke with what dignity I could muster: 'I have not yet seen *your* teeth, madame.'

Her peal of laughter sent a cloud of weaver birds whirring from the umbrella trees bordering the compound. She released the clip on the chain and the ape shot up the mango tree, yattering angrily. Her name, she told me when she had recovered somewhat, was Dorothy, but everyone called her the Monkey Woman. She hailed from Conakry, far to the north, and she had been visiting relatives at a nearby village when she had met François, the young harbour pilot whom I had come to visit. It had, as usual, been love at first sight for the impulsive Frenchman and he had invited her back to his house, where she had, by now, become firmly established.

She and François had hit it off from the start. Indeed, when the less snooty of the expatriate wives had recovered from their initial shock she had got on well with them too, mainly because she was quite uninhibited and full of salacious tales about the inadequacies and iniquities of the customers she had met during the course of her work in the dives of the metropolis.

It struck me as odd that such a friendly and vivacious

person as the Monkey Woman should have adopted such a repulsive companion as the ape. She had had him – for a 'him' he all too obviously was – for years and he accompanied her everywhere. I have never been overfond of the monkey breed at the best of times, and this particular specimen seemed to me to be in possession of even fewer endearing qualities than most of his kind. His proper name, she informed me, was Marmaduke, given to him many years previously by an English owner of dubious taste and humour. François, no doubt for good reasons of his own, had rechristened the creature 'Laval', after the reviled French traitor, and the name had stuck.

Laval was an ape of advanced years. Although scientifically he was, in fact, of a species known to scientists as a Guinea baboon, one of the smaller varieties of baboon, everything about him looked big enough to me. Especially his teeth. The handsome brown coat normally sported by the younger members of his species had gone, though, to be replaced now in his autumnal years by a mangy faecal-grey pelage. Large patches of hair were missing from all over his body, and the skin thus exposed looked as though it were afflicted by some rare and hideous disease.

He was moving through the branches of the tree now, still yakking his displeasure. He began to hurl mangoes at me, viciously and with increasing accuracy, rockets of things that fairly sang through the air. I moved well away. The Monkey Woman followed me. Laval retired to the top branches, glaring in our direction, his yells increasing in tempo and in volume. We watched in silence for a few minutes, then the Monkey Woman turned to me. 'He's jealous,' she said accusingly, 'and I think you're frightening the poor dear. Let's go inside and have a cold beer.'

I came to know Laval quite well over the next few months, and nothing he ever did made me feel any better about him. His approach to life was of the most rudimentary: if a thing moved, it was either for eating or for copulating with. He was, in addition, a tireless thief. He got drunk on whatever alcohol he could pilfer, and his craving for cigarettes – a habit acquired from the Monkey Woman – almost tripled François's monthly tobacco bill by the end of their first week of association. Garden employees left their lunch bowls untended at their peril: a regular sight during any working week would be Laval haring for the safety of the surrounding bush with a container of food under his arm, followed by a hail of missiles and bellows of wrath from his victim.

He was a creature of extremely liberal sexual proclivities. Any living thing found around his patch could consider itself a natural target for Laval's depraved libido. Goats that regularly grazed the grass around the edge of the compound received daily attention from him, a matter of complete indifference to the goats themselves but a source of huge irritation to their elderly herdsman, who had to endure endless ribald commentary from itinerant market women and small children about the deplorable moral standards of his charges. Dogs tied by their owners outside the port houses were simply asking for it, captive houris just waiting to be had as far as the ape was concerned.

His was a decidedly confrontational attitude with the human race. With the sole exception of the Monkey Woman, he hated them all. But he was capable of making exceptions to suit his own ends, as was proved on one memorable occasion when a gaggle of Carmelite nuns came visiting the French quarters in port. Laval – fortunately, it was to transpire – was secured to the long chain attached to the mango tree in anticipation of their visit; fortunately, it must be emphasised, because the sight of so many females garbed in their black and white religious vestments before him drove him into a veritable frenzy of eroticism. The divertissement he performed for the good Sisters from the lower branches of the mango tree that sunny afternoon must have been the talking point of their convent for rather a long time afterwards.

But possibly Laval's finest hour came on the day that Beatrice, a huge and lanky sow belonging to the paramount chief – a man not renowned for his liking of either baboons or Frenchmen – wandered innocently into the French compound. This was Beatrice's first time here and indeed it was her first time anywhere much, for she was the chief's prize sow and he kept her well and truly fenced in at his little farm a mile or so up the road. But she had broken out in a moment of boredom when no one was looking. The great big unexplored world beckoned, adventure stirred in her veins, the heavens were of their bluest, and Beatrice trotted off down the road. Stopping here and there to rootle happily among patches of cassava and yams and to sniff at horrible things, she eventually found herself down at the port. Reaching the gates of the French compound, she stopped abruptly. The heady smell of fermenting mangoes, a fruit of which she was passionately fond, came wafting over her. With a little grunt of sheer pleasure, she followed her nose through the gates and came to a halt under the mango tree.

The ground under the tree was littered with fallen fruit. It was a banquet fit for any pig of refined taste. Whuffling ecstatically, she put her nose to the ground and got stuck into what promised to be the feast of a lifetime. The first mango vanished in jig-time. The second had barely reached her oesophagus when Laval dropped upon her from the heavens.

Pigs, even African pigs, are creatures of habit. So long as they get much more than enough food at their disposal to keep body and soul together during their working day, they are usually content with life. They sleep the sleep of the just at night. It is true that love, such as we of the human race know it, is an emotion that rarely, if ever, touches their heart; they love their food and they love their sleep, and that's about it. The mating process, the nearest that the great and noble family of pigs get to our conception of love, is for the production of little piglets, and no more than that. Their consorts know nothing of the joys of foreplay, and they, for their part, want none of it either.

But there is a limit, even for the most easy-going of sows. Beatrice had led a sheltered life. In a short and generally humdrum career she had never known lust so intense that unidentified creatures would drop from on high to have her. And she had certainly never, ever, been mounted by a baboon. Knocked to the ground by the impetus, she scrambled to her feet, dazed and a bit winded, casting one shocked glance over her shoulder to see what had felled her. It was her first ever sight of a baboon, and she instantly prayed to God it would be her last. Laval's face, never considered even in the world of baboons to be anything other than ugly, looked like a vision from hell. Emitting a blood-curdling scream she took off at fifty miles per hour, heading for anywhere, just anywhere, away from this awful place and this awful THING clutching at her fundaments. When last seen by the hugely entertained audience of white Frenchmen and

black Africans, she was vanishing in a cloud of dust up the
road and still giving tongue with the unique delivery of pigs
the world over when the stresses of life become too much
for them. Laval, bouncing like a jockey on her rump and
enjoying himself more than he had done in a long time, was
still firmly ensconced within her.

In an attempt to guide Laval's carnal proclivities into
more socially acceptable channels, François bought Sushi
from a local trader. Sushi was a cute little white-nosed
guenon monkey with great big trusting eyes. She was not,
however, so naive as to trust Laval, and she rejected his
advances peremptorily. He ate her, down to the last cute
little tarsal bone.

Laval's sole redeeming quality was his undoubted affection for his mistress. He followed the Monkey Woman
everywhere, and one word from her was enough to curb
whatever excesses he happened to be wallowing in at the
time. His jealousy of François bordered on the maniacal,
and only a combination of François's boot and the Monkey
Woman's displeasure kept him from venting his spleen on
the Frenchman in a physical way.

It was François's astonishing revelation that Laval could
fish that led me to take a closer interest in the disgusting pri-
mate. 'He likes canoes,' the Frenchman told me. 'He won't go
out to sea, though, because he's too smart for that. He knows
that given half a chance I'd sling the bugger overboard for
the barracudas. But he loves it when we go out in the
swamps in the boat – I think maybe he feels more secure
when he sees trees around him. And he's keen on the fishing
part, too. I think it must have been the Englishman who first
owned him who trained him. We bait his hook and he sits in
the stern, fishing. And he seems to bring us luck, for when

he's out with us we always come back with a boatload of fish.'

This I just had to see. The Monkey Woman's relatives lived about two hours' trek into the swamps west of the port and I needed no encouragement to accept the invitation to join her, François and Laval on their next trip. It was the dry season, fortunately, so the water was never more than knee deep anywhere along the path. Laval bounded along on all fours ahead of us, sending water spraying in all directions, but never venturing far from our sight. Like all creatures who have spent most of their lives in human company, he had an innate distrust of the bush – in this case, probably well founded, for there were leopards in this area and they have a strong liking for baboon flesh. Where the waters became a bit deeper he swam behind us with a rapid sort of doggy-paddling stroke.

At first the vegetation was scrubby, varying from clumps of mangroves to thorny vines and reeds. Gradually taller trees began to appear until, eventually, we were passing through stands of giant red ironwoods. Wisps of mist filtered through the branches far above us and in the spooky gloom Laval, taking no chances, stayed close to the Monkey Woman.

Just before we arrived at our destination we came upon a broad stretch of very deep water. It was here that we encountered that West African phenomenon known as the floating bridge. This consisted of a narrow line of very long, thin wooden poles laid from one bank to the other and resting on the water surface, tied together with highly inadequate-looking liane. The moment a person stepped on to this bridge the poles sagged beneath the surface. The further one walked across the deeper they sagged, so that by the time one was halfway across the water was knee deep. What with the surrounding gloom and the murkiness of the water it became quite impossible to see the poles under us and it was necessary to feel one's way very carefully over it with the feet. There being no handrail of any sort and the underwater poles being very slippery, it made for a horrendous crossing. How the Monkey Woman managed, goodness only knows, for she not only had to piggy-back a petrified Laval across but she also had to hold the hand of an equally nervous Frenchman. Had she had a spare hand, she could probably have held mine, too.

The little fishing village consisted of five wooden huts sited precariously on stilts over the water. We stayed two nights there, I in a room in the chief's hut and the others with the Monkey Woman's relatives. The nights were made an utter misery by clouds of mosquitoes, and I hoped that Laval was getting his full share of them. In such proximity to the water, there was a soggy feel about everything and the smell of fish was constantly in the air. Mist hung thick over the water's edge under the trees, and one had to get well out on the water before one emerged into the sunshine. All in all it was rather a depressing place, and I would have had quite enough of it by the end of my first night had it not been for Laval.

An astonishing transformation had taken place in the ape. His whole personality had changed. Gone was the odious creature constantly on the lookout for trouble. Now his behaviour was almost civilized. He sat patiently on the little verandah of the hut, looking out over the water, waiting his turn to be fed, even allowing the children to scratch his back. Gone was the cunning, shifty look from the wicked eyes. Now they gazed upon the world with all the benignity of an Anglican archbishop.

But the greatest personality change was when he was out in the canoe. The village lived almost entirely by fishing, smoking or drying what they caught, then taking their catch to the outside markets. The waters around the village were teeming with fish and the canoes were out all day long. Most of the fishing was by net and trap and spear, but Laval eschewed such base tactics. For Laval had become One Of Us.

He would perch on the platform at the stern of the canoe like a little old man, line in hand and the end wrapped around his wrist for extra security. He sat with that look of resigned patience on his face that has always been the hall-mark of the true fisherman, his eyes never leaving the wooden float tied to the line, waiting for it to vanish under the water surface at the first snatch at the bait.

It was rarely long in coming. When the float disap-peared from view and the line jerked violently in his hand he would come to life instantly. A loud, triumphant HOO! would burst from him and he would wind the line in rapidly hand over hand until the fish lay gasping in the bottom of the canoe. Laval would never actually touch it himself – an early experience, resulting in a hook being embedded in his flesh, had convinced him that all fish were equipped with barbed iron fangs. But he knew what to do with his catch when he had it. He kept a lump of wood by him in the canoe and he would use this to good effect, methodically pounding the unfortunate fish until all life was extinct. Once it stopped moving he lost all interest in it, leaving the removal of the hook to others more adept.

The Monkey Woman had bought him a floppy sun bonnet to wear while he was out in the canoe. 'Monkeys,' she retorted indignantly when I laughed at the sight of him wearing it, 'can get sunstroke too.' The bonnet was a lemon-coloured thing with frilly edging and a blue forget-me-not motif, with pink ribbons that tied under his chin. He looked ludicrous but very smug in it, and he obviously thought he was the cat's whiskers when he had it on.

Whether Laval brought the villagers luck by his presence must be considered a moot point. Where fish are plentiful, good fishermen generally make their own luck. It is certainly a fact that, on the only two occasions on which I went out in a canoe containing Laval, we returned laden. It is also an undisputed fact that Laval was an honoured guest at the village, treated like a king, an accolade certainly never bestowed upon him anywhere else that I knew of. He was respected there, and, in return, he gave them respect by his exemplary behaviour.

Perhaps there is a moral there somewhere for all of us.

Laval's end was predictably violent. A contretemps with the Frenchman resulted in his assassination. I helped the Monkey Woman bury him in the bush beyond the compound. She stuck a rough wooden cross over his grave and chanted a prayer to the Lord of all Apes, beseeching Him to guide Laval's evil, cantankerous soul through the celestial swamps. Immediately afterwards she boarded a mammy waggon and departed, never to be seen or heard of again.

'Her prayers were wasted,' remarked the Frenchman when she had gone. 'If there's a hell for apes, that's where that bastard will be.'

I am not so sure myself. Whatever a person's sins have been in life, there is, I believe, always hope in eternity for a fisherman. Indeed, when my own time eventually comes and I am paddling my way through the Heavenly

Everglades, it would not greatly surprise me to meet at some peaceful anabranch another celestial canoe, bearing on the platform at its stern Laval, complete with forget-me-not bonnet and trolling for angelfish.

After all, Christ Himself was a bit of a fisherman, and fishermen tend to look after their own.

4

When Life Gets Tedious

The sun gets up and the sun goes down,
The hands of the clock keep moving around,
You're no sooner up than it's time to lie down –
Life gets teejus, don't it?

Peter Lynd Hayes

When depression wraps her icy claws around your weary soul; when nerves are taught as piano wire and the ends are sticking out through the follicles of your skin like fish-hooks; when your mind is wallowing in the darkest recesses of hell itself; when you find Jehovah's Witnesses dogging your footsteps ever more vigilantly with each passing day, imploring you to jump aboard their celestial bus before it is too late; when even the Samaritans can offer you no cheer other than to advise you to use good old-fashioned Irish linen because ordinary hempen rope tends to chafe the neck a bit when you make that final plunge: do not give up the ghost just yet. There is still hope. There are places, sanctuaries even, still remaining on this great, unfeeling world of ours, where life's cruel flails can no more assail you. They may be far, far away and they will certainly not be easy to find but, if you are of a sufficiently persevering nature you will make it.

But a word of warning: it will behove you naught to approach your local travel agents. Excellent though they may be at arranging flights and cruises to the world's more popular – and most populous – holiday resorts, these are not for you. Peace and quiet is what you want. If the sort of destination you have in mind is one that is familiar to the travel agents, avoid it.

The first place you should visit, therefore, is your local library. Even relatively small libraries stock quite large world atlases. Browse through those. If you are a sunshine addict, you will naturally concentrate on the hot countries. If, however, the thought of all that sunshine depresses you even further, the colder regions of the world will be for you. Study carefully those great blank patches still to be found even on the most modern of maps, those intriguing areas of nothing on which, in my youth, I kept expecting to find inscribed the caution 'Here be dragons'. Take your pick. If you are so fortunate as to have a large bank balance, you can travel in style to the port of call nearest to your choice before strapping your rucksack on your back and plodding off into oblivion. If, however, austerity in its harsher forms is more suited to your budget and your frame of mind then you can still, I am led to believe, work your passage on certain vessels. And allow yourself not to be put off by the fact that a disturbingly high percentage of those seem to be under Liberian registration – inflatable rubber life jackets, complete with whistle and dinky little flashing red light, can be purchased quite cheaply at most ports before you depart. (Under no circumstances put your faith in the few standard issue lifebelts you may see hanging on the rails of such vessels; these will have been made around the time of the Crimean War and will have about the same degree of buoyancy as the ship's anchor.) Whalers, for example, still operate within the Laptev Sea on Siberia's northern fringes, and you can still find the occasional coal wherry plying the lonely, watery wastes off the coasts of Namibia and Mauritania. You will have all the austerity you crave on each of these types of vessel, and surely rendering blubber – or whatever it is that one does with blubber – in sub-zero temperatures, or shovelling anthracite on and off a wherry at a hundred and twenty in the shade, is a small price to pay for free passage to the Shangri-la of your choice.

Shangri-la. 'A remote or imaginary utopia', my dictionary tells me. We each have our own, highly personal, view as to what that utopia should be like. Paradise in earthly form can appear in the most unlikely of places and situations. I think I have come close to finding my Shangri-la on a few occasions, and at no time did I have to shovel coal or hack blubber from dead leviathans to get to any of them. Big-hearted employers actually paid me to work in them.

For several months I lived on the fringe of an African leper colony. It was one of the most pleasant and peaceful chapters of my life. There were no postal services, no bills, no junk mail, no insurance representatives flogging annuities or London wide boys trying to sell stolen carpets, no rapists, no muggers, no child molesters, no do-gooders; none, in fact, of those little irritations we are supposed to accept as being part and parcel of the price we must pay for living in civilized societies. In this leper colony there was an absence of *Homo sapiens var. alba*, and indeed a satisfactory absence of the subspecies anywhere else within forty square miles around us. My neighbours were many, but they were black to the last man, woman and child. Many, of course, were lepers, but, both as neighbours and as friends, I found them to be of a considerably higher standard than a great many others I have had perforce to associate with in more 'advanced' societies.

The New Hope leprosy mission lay between the main Cape Palmas to Webbo road and the Grand Cess River in Liberia. As it was only about fifteen miles inland from the ocean the land on which it was sited was low-lying. It was crisscrossed by many creeks, most of them small, and the soil, being alluvial, was deep and fertile; despite the relatively flat topography, it was surprisingly well drained and so even throughout the dry season it retained moisture without the usual water stagnation.

It would perhaps be more accurate to say that at the time of my visit New Hope *had* been a leprosy mission, for it was no longer officially in business as such. It had been built in the 1920s by American missionaries and had remained a very active mission until quite recent times, when a long-standing land ownership dispute between the missionaries and the indigènes had led to such hostility that the former had eventually packed up their gear and returned to the United States. Now not one of the missionaries remained, at least none of the living ones, for the many graves in the large cemetery behind the village gave poignant testimony to those who had left their bones behind in the belief of the righteousness of their cause.

I had not arrived with any belief in the righteousness of

my cause. Large stands of virgin mahogany forest had been
reported in the vicinity of New Hope and, as the area fell
within the concession boundary of some Danish timber
exploiters who were held in great favour by the government
of the day, I had been asked to do a complete assessment of
species and logging potential. I had been given a dozen
porters-cum-tracecutters to help out.

The road into New Hope from the main Cape Palmas
road had been built and maintained by the missionaries. At
one time it had obviously been an excellent one. With the
missionaries gone it had fallen into considerable disrepair,
with bridges washed away and the jungle creeping back in.
It was now nothing but a rutted track, quite impassable to
any form of vehicle, and at times degenerating into no more
than a footpath. We therefore walked the twelve miles in
from the main road, the crew carrying our 'loads' on their
heads. We met no one. This at one time had been coastal
rainforest, but now the big trees had gone, removed either
by the missionaries for building purposes or by subsistence
farmers. Only the very occasional tall ironwood was to be
seen sticking forlornly above the low tangles of vegetation
that had taken over the tracts of abandoned farmland on
either side of the road. The resultant uninterrupted sunshine brought out hordes of multi-hued butterflies to feed
upon rotting rubbish at the road verges, and their fat green
caterpillars to swarm over the leaves of wild banana and
paw-paw wherever we looked.

Bird life abounded. Hornbills croaked their harsh call
among the thickets, taking off in clumsy swishing flight as
we approached, only to crash-land in the bushes a little way
down the track to gawp at us. Red, black and yellow weavers
squabbled in the wild oil palms, paying not the slightest

attention to us, and flocks of tiny waxbills fed on seeding grasses everywhere. A large, fat cassava snake, basking in the middle of the road, hissed his explosive, lethal warning at us, only to be despatched by one of the crew with a machete, and a lovely little duiker antelope got the fright of his life when he emerged timidly from the roadside scrub and saw us marching in single file towards him. He bounded high in the air with a snort of alarm and vanished in the blink of an eye.

I had, of course, been made aware by my employers before departure to New Hope that the area had, at one time, been a very active leper colony and that there was still a remnant of it remaining. However I had neglected to mention this fact to my workers, assuming that they already knew and were not too bothered about it. I could not have been more wrong. They were horrified. Immediately upon discovering the dread news, only the fact that I instantly promised them a substantial increase in wages and guaranteed them that we would give the village and its inhabitants a wide berth kept them from marching straight back out again. Oddly enough, they weren't bothered about the fact that I would have to maintain a good relationship with the lepers – their belief that my 'white man's juju' would protect me from all sickness was absolute. They set up camp in an old abandoned farm full of cassava, yams and plantains gone wild, well away from the leper colony, while I walked on down the path to establish contact with the villagers and try to find sleeping quarters for myself.

I rounded a corner and suddenly I seemed to have entered a different, magical world. The riot of vegetation all around had gone and I was gazing across a vast and lovely sward of close-cropped grass. At the far end of it half a dozen

little black African cows grazed peacefully and, beyond
them, a silver glint of water under the shade of a bank of tall,
dark trees could just be seen. Dappled shadows from the tall
flame tree to the left of the compound flitted and danced
over the roof of a large mud-block bungalow, its neatly
whitewashed walls and the corrugated iron sheeting of its
roof proclaiming to all the affluence of its owner. The flame
tree was in full bloom, and the spread of its flat crown over
the house was a glorious vision in scarlet. Yellow-flowering
cassia bushes, also in full flower, were scattered all over the
compound, and a huge spiky lemon bush was providing
shade from the noonday sun for the small flock of ruminat-
ing sheep and goats lying under it. The rich fragrance of the
creamy-white lemon blossom came wafting over me, the
heady scent so powerful as to almost, but not quite, suppress
the pungent aroma of hot African goat.

A short distance from the house stood a solitary breadfruit tree, its big green fruit hanging like cannonballs from
the branches. Although rather similar in appearance to the
breadfruit tree of fame and fable, the African version is different in a number of respects. The true breadfruit, of the
Artocarpus species, although grown extensively nowadays
throughout the Pacific and the Caribbean is native to neither
place, having spread from Asia to the tropical South Seas in
prehistoric times. The African breadfruit, *Treculia africana*,
has migrated nowhere, having stayed right where it
belonged in tropical Africa. It belongs to, as the botanical
name shows, a different genus and its normal habitat is the
rainforest, being cultivated but rarely on the outskirts of villages. The relative straightness of stem of the Pacific variety
means that the timber is widely used for carpentry and the
making of canoes, and a rough cloth is made from its fibrous

inner bark. There are no such uses for the African breadfruit: so grossly fluted is its trunk that no use at all can be made of its timber other than firewood, and it is not even much use for that.

The leaves of both species look alike, being large and fan-shaped. The fruits, too, are very similar in outer appearance, being huge, heavy, green globes, spherical in shape but with large surface nodules, and they can be anything up to twelve inches in diameter. But again, here the similarity ends. In the Pacific and the Caribbean it is the white fibrous pulp of the fruit that is eaten and for which the tree is named. (The pulp, when baked or cooked, is supposed to taste like bread.) In the African species it is the brown walnut-sized nuts contained within the pulp that are eaten and these are easily removed by the simple expedient of placing the whole fruit in a pool of water and allowing it to rot.

The only sign of life around the house was an arrogant old rooster and a collection of scrawny hens. The door and wooden window shutters were wide open, however, and I called out a greeting. The dull clunking of pestle in mortar started up behind the house. I went round and found a young girl, tiny infant strapped on her back, pounding yams. She looked up and stopped what she was doing, eyeing me without the slightest trace of curiosity. Her name was Alice, she said, and she was the wife of the local schoolmaster. This was their house. They had been expecting me, having received news of my impending arrival via a messenger sent through the bush by my employers. Her husband was away on business for a month, she informed me, but he had left instructions that she should prepare a room in the house for me. In fact, the whole place would be mine until he returned, she said, for she would be spending nights with her auntie over in the village.

She showed me my bedroom, a sparse but immaculately clean room containing an ancient iron bed on which lay a mattress of sacking stuffed with kapok. Meantime, in anticipation of my arrival she had purchased some tea and cans of milk on a recent visit to Cape Palmas, and if I would care for some now . . .?

I sat on a canvas deck chair by the door. The sun was sinking, casting long shadows over the compound. Behind the house the girl was heating a bucket of water over the fire for my bath. On another fire a large black pot emitting exotic fragrances was bubbling away. Only God and the girl knew what she was cooking for the evening meal, but I was feeling hungry already.

A cool zephyr ruffled the leaves of the breadfruit tree. Flights of grey parrots, fifty to a hundred birds at a time, soared high overhead, wheeling round and round, chattering and whistling endlessly. Every so often a raft of them would peel off from the main group and plummet down into the darkness of the trees beyond the water. I watched as they dropped down to their roosts, marvelling at the instinct that took them out to distant feeding places each morning, yet that unfailingly set them off at the same time each afternoon on the return journey to the roosting spots each had vacated that morning.

I gave the workers the following day off to allow them to organize their camp and explore their surroundings. The water I had glimpsed the previous evening beyond the compound turned out to be a wide but shallow stream. The wooden bridge that the missionaries had built over it had long since fallen down so I waded across. Alice was there and she took me to meet the chief, a jolly old chap with four fingers of his left hand missing. He was pleased to see me. The New Hope people would all be glad to learn of the timber men's interest in the area, he told me, for the loggers would have to repair the road and the bridges to get their timber out. Transport would once again be able to reach the village to carry its people to the outside markets and make it easier to bring in urgent medical supplies. Although the missionaries had gone, he said, the clinic was still operating on and off under government supervision. There was a clinic dispenser who could treat basic ailments and the less badly affected of the lepers, but when he needed any supplies from the outside world he had to walk out to get them. Lack of proper medical facilities had made many of the lepers turn to the old traditional native treatments.

He showed me round the old mission buildings. Most were in ruins, and the few that remained in any kind of shape were occupied by squatters. The missionaries had traded very extensively in crops such as oranges, avocados, cocoa and yams, no doubt, I assumed, in order to try to defray at least some of the operational costs of the running of the leper colony. Farm implements – even one tractor – now lay rusting and derelict behind the old workshops. Plantations of fruit trees stretched seemingly to infinity on the higher slopes behind the mission buildings, but they, too, had an air of sad neglect about them. The village women, the chief informed me, sold what fruit they could carry to the markets of Webbo and Cape Palmas, but there was such an abundance of it that most rotted where it had fallen from the trees.

'How much do they get for the oranges at the markets outside?' I asked curiously. 'Forty cents per hundred,' he replied, 'and the women, don't forget, have to carry their produce every inch of the way out to the main road.'

The lepers were unfailingly cheerful and friendly. Most of the ones I saw were only slightly affected by the disease, but some were in really poor condition. A few were downright revolting to look at, faces half eaten by the sickness. One old lady who was obviously in its terminal stages had the remaining stump of her arm covered by a horrible liquid putrescence, yet she managed to smile at me and greet me with the traditional West African 'Wel-i-come, massa, wel-i-come' from her sleeping mat in the corner of her hut. It required quite an effort on my part not to show revulsion when looking at flesh eaten away to the bone by this ghastly disease, but they made it so much easier through the wonderful expressions, the outstretched hands, the obvious warmth shown to me, a white stranger suddenly come into their midst. Those who had come in from the outside for such treatment as was currently available at the little clinic had brought their wives and families with them, and these relatives tended to the victim's domestic needs uncomplainingly, quite resigned to the fact that they themselves stood a good chance of becoming afflicted. 'If we get sick, it is because it has been ordained by God,' was their philosophical response.

The old man took me to the mission graveyard. There were many graves, each adorned with a simple cement headstone. Most had been men, but some of the graves contained women. All had been teachers, agriculturalists and medical staff from the United States. Most had been in their early twenties when they died. There was nothing on their headstones to indicate the cause of death, but I reflected that there must have been plenty of potentially fatal illnesses around in this part of Africa to choose from in the 1930s.

One of the more recent graves was that of a twenty-one-year-old pilot. The old man pointed to a huge old silk-cotton tree towering above the forest to the right of us. The missionaries had built an airstrip to bring in urgent medical supplies, he said, and they had purchased a small single-engined plane from America. The pilot, too, had been hired from the States and had lived in the mission. He had been a popular young man with everyone. No one ever found out what had caused the accident, for it had been a beautifully clear evening with no wind at all when he came in to land. The wing of the plane had clipped the top of the cotton tree, and that had been that. Shortly after that, the missionaries, tired of the escalating land dispute and the constant toll in life, had packed up and gone home, never to return.

We walked down the valley and through what had been the old mission farmlands. Initially the whole area had been a massive swamp that had been drained by the missionaries and turned into pastures for cattle and arable land for the growing of rice, yams and cassava. Where there had once been orderly fields, now there was just a jungle of scrub and sawgrass. The irrigation ditches were still to be seen, but they were gradually becoming clogged up and it was obvious that it would only be a matter of time before the whole area reverted to its former state of stagnant swampland. The people had neither the expertise nor the will to do anything about the situation, said the chief. Everything was in the lap of God with them. Even for those who were perfectly fit, it was easier to pray than to grab a shovel and do some work.

What instantly struck me was the incredible numbers of pied kingfishers here. There must have been thousands of them, blackbird-sized birds, everywhere, clustered on shrubs, swooping into the ditches, and on speeding overhead wings. It was a truly magnificent sight.

To those readers who have never seen this charming bird, the information that its feathers are of a simple black and white coloration might perhaps make the pied kingfisher sound rather plebeian when compared to the other, more familiar, members of the great kingfisher family with their multi-hued cloaks. But the pied kingfisher is stunningly beautiful. This is a masterpiece crafted in black and white: the Greta Garbo of the bird world, with undergarments of the purest of white and upper parts of the most startling black and white patterning. In this place the birds were in the ideal setting to show off their beauty to the best advantage. They were constantly on the move, and the glossy obsidian-black and pristine white of their plumage was a shimmering, shifting marvel against the cloudless delicate blue mantle of the heavens and the lush, mottled green of the fields. It created the surreal impression of witnessing a magical flying carpet from the fables of ancient Araby in which no colour remained constant, in which nothing remained constant except the aura of absolute peace with which the viewer became imbued through watching this wonderful spectacle of nature.

The air resounded to their vibrant whistles and shrill 'kwik-kik-kik' cries. 'The ditches are full of frogs and crayfish,' explained the chief, 'and that is mostly what we eat, too. There is a belief among us that so long as the kingfishers remain we will survive as a people, for the crayfish will still be here. They are our luck birds.'

Luck birds. How apt, I mused. The ancient Greeks, too, considered them so. They had many legends about the kingfisher, lovely, tranquil legends. After all, their word for the bird, *alkuon*, gave the English language *halcyon*, meaning peace and happiness.

The following day I went into the forest beyond the mission with my crew. It was certainly virgin coastal rainforest, but it soon became apparent to me that, from the commercial logger's point of view, the forest was worthless. I had not been more than half a day walking through it when I knew in my heart that the concessionaires would not find one stick of mahogany in it, nor indeed any other marketable species. It consisted almost entirely of a species quite unknown to the world of timber and but vaguely known even to the world of dendrology, a species recognized by me as being one grandly labelled by scientists as *Didelotia brevanipaniculata*. I had only seen it once before myself and I had never seen its timber, for even the bush Africans considered the wood to be useless. It was, however, a splendid-looking tree, tall and straight and with glowing red bark, and there must have been many thousands of them there in that relatively modest area of forest. However, regardless of my initial prognosis, I still had to map the whole area and do a full-scale tree enumeration, so I knew that I had several months' work ahead of me before the task was completed.

The forest was as peaceful as the lands beyond its boundaries. None of the larger land predators had entered it in the memory of man. This was fishing country. Great white-caped fishing eagles patrolled the overhead skies, dividing their time between the waters of the forest and the sea to the south. Bands of monkeys chattered in the tree canopy and orioles glittered in glorious gold in the shades of the lower branches. It was the dry season, and there was unremitting sunshine, but it was never at any time an oppressive heat. The feathery foliage of the tall trees allowed the sunlight to percolate gently and kindly down to the forest floor, and the fresh sea breezes from the Atlantic, by now considerably throttled down after filtering through the mangroves of the coastal regions, were a pleasantly invigorating influence as we worked.

Alice's husband finally arrived, a tall, rather taciturn man, somewhat gloomy and introspective. I saw little of him; he and I were working by day, and at night he mostly retired to his own quarters or went off to visit friends in the village. I asked Alice if she was not afraid that they would catch the disease. 'He already has it,' she replied quietly. 'On his body, under his shirt. That is why we are here – we were driven from our home town because of it. It begins with lumps on the body, and goes on from there.'

'But aren't you afraid for yourself and your child . . .?' I began.

'I have got the lumps now too,' she said without looking at me. 'I discovered them last week.'

I was at a loss for words. She picked up the pestle and turned away from me. 'It is God's will,' she said. The pestle thumped woodenly in the mortar. The child strapped to her back was sound asleep, its head bobbing up and down in time to the rhythm.

The breadfruit tree was a roosting point for a pair of kingfishers. Every evening they would come to preen themselves on a dead branch near the top, their plumage shining in the setting sun. I was intrigued to note that the tree's leaves perspired constantly and copiously, large globules of moisture falling from them in a regular shower bath of water, keeping the ground around the base of the tree permanently damp. It did this every dry season, Alice informed me, and stopped when the rains began.

Quite often Alice would add some of the breadfruit nuts to her stews of crayfish and freshwater crabs. Sometimes the nuts would be cooked and added whole, and sometimes she would pound them to a paste in her mortar to add to the stew as a thickener. Either way, they were delicious, imparting a sort of groundnut flavour to the meal.

Those were magical times. Peaceful days, peaceful evenings, peaceful nights. The sound of the surf was never too far away as we worked in the forest, while the tang of the sea purged the air of its natural stickiness and kept the mosquitoes at bay as I slept. The evenings, too, were bliss. There was time then to daydream, time to think without interruption at the end of a day's work as I lay back in my deck chair in front of the house watching the kingfishers. There was only the strangely soporific pounding of the pestle and the crackle of the cooking fire and the distant call of the parrots to intrude upon my lazy thoughts, and I could have happily gone on to the end of my time in this environment . . .

The workers were singing as they packed their gear. It was the morning of departure and they were glad of it, delighted to be returning to the outside world, to the stenches and cacophonous rackets of their version of civilization, eagerly anticipating the opportunity of squandering their earnings on beer and tobacco and fine clothing with which to impress their doxies in the urban dives. The sea breeze had gone and the air was oppressively muggy, the usual prelude to the rain season.

We had travelled about six miles when I called a halt by a pretty little stream flowing across the track. The workers put down their loads gratefully and drank from its waters before sitting at the roadside to engage in idle chit-chat.

A movement caught my eye a short distance upstream from us. A kingfisher was preening himself at the end of a dead branch overhanging the water. The black and white patterning of his plumage gleamed in the morning light.

He stopped to peer at us, the little black crest on his head twitching up and down, the sun reflecting in a laser-point of light from the centre of his coal-black eye. Then suddenly he launched himself from his perch into rapid flight. He circled over us once, climbing higher and higher into the pastel-blue of the sky, before heading due west in the direction of New Hope. I kept gazing at the western horizon until long after he had vanished from my sight.

My carriers had disappeared round the bend, moving swiftly eastward towards the main road, anxious to be away from New Hope and its accursed lepers. I sighed deeply, then I turned my back to the west, moving away from the woodpeckers and from my Shangri-la.

5

The Black Madonna

Remote parts of the world have always fascinated me. As a child I would pore endlessly over atlases, gazing at strange names in strange places, pondering about them, dreaming about them, wondering about the people who lived in them, what it was that made their present inhabitants decide that this was their Shangri-la. Why was Black Diamond in the Rockies so named? And Bloodvein River in Manitoba? What terrible rites of witchcraft were being enacted in Liberia's Sasstown and in Nigeria's Ikot Ekpene even as I daydreamed? What did the people of the Russian steppes do for entertainment when their long day's toil was over? Did they, in fact, have *any* forms of entertainment to occupy their leisure hours? Did they even have *any* leisure hours? What could possibly have attracted the very first settlers to bleak and inhospitable lands such as Tierra del Fuego, Patagonia and Mongolia? And would I ever be able to find out any of the answers for myself when I grew older?

Such musings exercised my juvenile mind on rainy nights, of which there were plenty during the long Galloway winters. I have never, alas, been able to make the journey to the southern extremity of the Americas or to Mongolia, nor do I ever expect to do so now. In any case, desire to visit those lands faded at a fairly early stage when I discovered the former to be the home of llamas and the latter to be infested with camels, both species having already been placed high on my list of Creatures I Can Well Do Without the moment I discovered their revolting propensity for expectorating fluidly and copiously upon anyone to whom they take a dislike. (This trait was effectively demonstrated on my first trip to Africa when a dromedary plastered my beautiful new palm-beach suit from collar to ankle with a stippling of evil-smelling Nile-green slime at Tripoli Airport.)

Nor have I ever been seriously tempted to visit the Russian steppes. For one thing pictures of those honest peasant women, brawny of limb and homely of visage, whose exploits as tank commanders against the Nazi invaders in the 1940s stirred the world, somehow never managed to ignite the latent embers of lust ever ready to explode into flame within the MacIntosh engine-room. Steel false teeth and hirsute armpits may have excited the libido of the sturdy shepherds of the Russian plains, but a youthful diet of Betty Grable and Esther Williams in the Whithorn Picture House had refined my own ideas of true feminine pulchritude almost to the meretricious.

In the end, though, it was neither the shortcomings of the camels nor the women that kept me away from the more far-flung of those places. Mainly, it was the trees. Or rather, the dearth of them. My father had been associated with trees all of his life, and I suppose I had inherited his love of them. A life without trees around me was quite unthinkable.

There was, too, the craving for adventure. This was even stronger within me than it appeared to be in many of my peers, most of whom seemed happy enough to hang around the home environment, and there was the ever growing suspicion that there were certain parts of the world in which the sort of excitement I craved might be rather hard to find. This was encouraged by my reading matter at the time. The *Hotspur*, the *Wizard*, the *Adventure* and the *Dandy* never seemed to carry stories about, for example, Boris from Nizhnyaya Tunguska or Bakmounth from Ulan Bator. It is true that, on occasion, those excellent publications would feature home-grown heroes like Wild Young Dirky and Cripple Dick, but most of the adventure stories that interested me tended to occur in places such as Africa and Canada, countries in which the names used were at least pronounceable. For some reason not quite clear to me even now, I rather favoured Africa in those days. As childhood progressed into adolescence the desire to travel to the Dark Continent became ever stronger, so that by the time I had reached manhood the wish to see for myself the great mahogany forests of the White Man's Grave had become overpowering. It was inevitable that I should eventually go there, and when I did so I found the great, brooding forests to be everything I could have wished for, with more adventure on a daily basis than one could shake a stick at. What I had not bargained for, however, was the fact that where you had rainforest, you also had to put up with the swamps that had helped create them.

For someone who has spent a disproportionate part of

his life up to the waist and beyond in their murky waters, it
might be considered a contradiction in terms that I should
express revulsion for swamps. But this is a fact. Swamps are
among my least favourite places in the whole world. Anyone
wishing to sponsor me on a trip to the Florida Everglades
could be assured of a rather dusty response. I have never
been there, and I hope to God I never go. Let the travel
brochures drool on as they wish about the charms of those
watery expanses. I know better. I have, as it were, been tried
in the furnace. While I have no doubt that from the air-
conditioned luxury of the average holiday launch the
combination of sunshine, limpid waters and egret-lined
banks may, to the casual visitor, make this a tourist's heaven,
let that same tourist take a stroll on deck to admire the setting of the sun beyond the mangrove swamps. Or, better
still, let him plunge overboard to enjoy a refreshing swim in
their waters.

For one thing that the travel brochures rarely reveal is
that anywhere in the world vast quantities of swamp water
generally mean vast quantities of bloodsucking insects. Even
the more northerly latitudes are seldom free from those
voracious pests: Siberia and Labrador are host to some of the
biggest and most savagely aggressive mosquitoes in the
world, great big long-legged beasties with syringes designed
to penetrate the hides of the oldest and toughest of moose
and caribou bulls. And swamp waters are usually crawling
with obscenely long, slithery, carnivorous creatures that just
do not bear thinking about. Everything, but everything,
above or below the waters of a swamp either stings or bites.
And a not inconsiderable proportion of the underwater population of tropical swamps are big enough to swallow a man
whole.

Tropical swamps are particularly unpleasant places. They are home to the dreaded anopheles mosquito, a tiny, black innocuous-looking chappie that is carrier of such nasty ailments as yellow fever, filaria, elephantiasis and three different types of malaria, all of them unpleasant. The equally lethal hordes of tsetse flies, emerging at dawn while the whine of the last nocturnal mosquito is still ringing tinnily in your eardrum, carries sleeping sickness, feasting on the blood of crocodiles, swamp antelopes and any human being unlucky enough to find himself within a ten-mile radius of their breeding range, while horseflies, carriers of anthrax and the common plague, also come out by the billion during daylight hours.

There is little rest for anyone whose circumstances force him to live in the middle of an African swamp. Clothing is no protection at all, and I have never known the mosquito net that was absolute proof against the mosquito. Somehow or other one will have managed to infiltrate your mosquito net as you climb into bed, no matter how careful you are, and it only makes its presence known when you are in that euphoric dream world between dozing and sleeping. There is nothing on earth more irritating. You are wide awake instantly and sleep is impossible from that point onward, for you spend the rest of the night trying to track down the wretched thing by the feeble light of torch or lantern, in the general upheaval almost inevitably allowing access to many more of its kind.

It is bad enough for those for whom canoes are a necessary mode of transport. Such travellers are a captive banquet just waiting to be devoured. Even worse was it for those like myself who had to spend a chunk of their lives wading through swamps. Apart from the sludge and the

stench and the snakes and the crocodiles, inland African
waters are chock-a-block with minute and deadly parasites.
Water-fleas, abundant everywhere, carry the larvae of the
horrific guinea worm, a thread-like worm that grows to
prodigious lengths inside the body before emerging, inch by
inch, through the skin to begin the alfresco part of its life
cycle. Water snails, also to be found by the legion in West
African waters, harbour the larvae of the tropical blood
fluke, a flatworm that lodges in the intestines and bladder.
Most enter the body through the natural orifices, but some
are so microscopic that they are quite capable of entering
through the pores of the skin.

And so on, practically ad infinitum. But swamps have
always been a major part of the geography of the Coast, and
they have always been the waters of life to many tribes and
many species of wildlife. Seemingly impervious to the dis-
comfort and the perpetual damp and the mosquitoes, tribes
such as the Nzima and the Arikam of the Ivory Coast erected
their deceptively fragile-looking houses of palm sticks on
slender bamboo stilts along the banks of the waterways on
which they fished, and the Igbos, who were among the earliest settlers of the Niger Delta, fashioned their famous long
canoes of supreme craftmanship from single tree trunks.
Massive pythons cruised through the foetid waters nightly,
while the harsh croaking of hornbills rang out daily among
the mangroves. On the patches of land that rose marginally
here and there from the ooze the peoples of the swamps
grew yams and cassava and peppers, and mongoose, civet
cat and leopard patrolled the animal tracks that weaved their
way through the tangles of vegetation, oblivious to the ticks
and the incessant rain. High above this watery wilderness
great flights of red-tailed parrots whistled their swift-winged,

mysterious ways at dawn and dusk, heading for God knew where, and that great, beautiful white-shawled pirate the fish eagle circled vigilantly overhead, forever on the lookout for easily intimidated predators such as the osprey and the goliath heron in order to bully them into releasing their catch for him.

It was not only the indigenous fishermen, however, who made use of the swamps in order to conduct their various businesses. White people used them too. It is true that one very rarely came across them in a day's travel, but they were there nevertheless. Now and again, as one drifted leisurely up some creek or other, one would suddenly and incongruously see a large, closely cropped rectangle of grass excised from the vegetal morass along the bank, with, at its highest point and well away from the waterside, a neat tin-roofed or palm-thatched house with whitewashed walls, a dwelling that, by the general air of neatness and orderliness surrounding it, proclaimed the fact that the occupant was unlikely to be other than expatriate. This would almost invariably be the home of a timber man, trader or missionary. If it stood on its own, it was more than likely to be that of the former, for timber men are notoriously shy creatures, seldom seeking the company of their fellow men. If on the outskirts of a village it was likely to be the trader or the missionary, for neither of those two, by the very nature of their calling, could afford to completely separate themselves from the hoi polloi.

Missionaries were indefatigable builders of schools and clinics in remote places, and to the African of the interior these were subjects close to the heart. In this field few could surpass the men from Rome, but there is a price to be paid for everything, as the bush Africans well knew, and they

paid theirs by having to accept the white man's religion as
part of the deal. Missions sprang up in the most unlikely of
places, the fishing villages of the creeks and swamps among
them. It was a lonely life and a harsh one for those young
priests who found themselves posted – usually on their own
insofar as other white people were concerned – to hot,
humid, rain-drenched hell-holes for tours that often lasted
four or five years at a time. But, as the majority were there
because they wanted to be, I rarely heard a complaint from
any of them.

The swamps of the Niger Delta were home to a number
of those missions. One such was based at Iteru. It was there
that the Reverend Father Patrick Sean O'Leary had set up
shop. And it was there that I first set eyes on the Black
Madonna.

For a month or more I had been messing around the
creeks and channels of this part of the Delta in a dugout
canoe, checking water depth for the possibility of future log
rafting and doing an inventory of the trees that grew on the
tiny islets and larger pockets of drier ground in this rather
forbidding world. Finding myself at last in a gloomy backwater that I recognized as being on the fringe of my old
friend Paddy's stamping ground, I decided to head for his
mission to escape from the torment of the insects for a few
days. Apart from that and the fact that I was getting pretty
tired of eating fish, everything I possessed was wet and filthy
and basic supplies needed replenishing. Added attractions
were that Paddy always managed to have a good supply of
imported beer in his paraffin refrigerator and that he was a
raconteur par excellence.

Paddy had opened the Iteru mission a few years previously. It was pretty isolated and was surrounded by water for

the greater part of the year. But the area was by no means sparsely populated; indeed, the town of Iteru was a thriving community and quite large by bush standards. From being a fairly ordinary fishing village in the 1930s it had developed quite suddenly into a prosperous town of several hundred inhabitants, mainly because of the fact that the drier and more fertile ground around it had proved ideal for the growing of cocoa.

One of Paddy's first tasks had been the building of a clinic and school and a house for himself. Behind his house he had begun the construction of a church, and this was now at the stage of having four walls and a roof but no windows or doors. It had been a slow process, as much of his building material had had to come in by canoe from the outside world. But the African's all-consuming desire to see his children properly educated had made the little school a resounding success from the beginning, and the tiny church, despite its incomplete state, was packed to overflowing whenever Paddy held Mass.

It was, in fact, a Sunday when I arrived, and Paddy had just returned from church. We were sitting on his verandah having our first beer of the day and waiting for his cook to prepare our meal when our reminiscences were interrupted by the appearance of a tall, slender girl standing outside the house, waiting courteously for permission to come up the verandah steps. Paddy signalled for her to enter.

She was a veritable black madonna, but she was not really black, either. Her skin was of a flawless, light-brown complexion, with what seemed to be an almost golden patina to it. Her features were not what one would have expected to find in this area, reminding one more of those of the graceful savannah Fulanis than of the more obviously

Negroid races of the Iteru swamps. She wore a European dress of some bright floral pattern, an unusual sight in itself in this remote part. She was, Paddy told me later, sixteen years of age, which made her a grown woman by bush standards. She was, quite simply, stunningly beautiful.

'Any news from the Bishop yet, Fadder?' she asked hesitantly.

'No, Caroline, no news yet,' replied my friend.

'Thank you, Fadder,' she said. She curtseyed gracefully to each of us, then was gone.

'Who,' I breathed in a mixture of astonishment and awe, 'was that?'

Paddy gazed at the girl's slowly retreating form for a moment or two before answering. 'That,' he replied softly, 'is Miss Caroline Ademugu.'

I watched as she walked down the hill towards the town. 'She certainly is remarkably beautiful,' I commented. 'What does she do?'

He held his glass up against the sun. A fly struggled in its death throes in the pale amber liquid. He hooked it out with his forefinger and flicked it out over the verandah rail.

'She's a whore,' replied the Reverend Father laconically.

'A WHAT?'

'You heard me – she's a whore!' And then, seeing me gazing speechless at him, disbelief written all over my face, he continued with relish: 'Let me explain the facts of life to you, me boy. Ever since Adam and Eve started mucking about with those mangoes in the Garden, this earth has been host to a certain type of lady, one who has decided from a very early age that not for her will life be one of unremitting drudgery for a generally ungrateful husband. The really lucky ones marry millionaires; others less fortunate hit the bright lights. These pragmatic young ladies have figured out that a much better use can be made of their natural assets by hiring them out on a very temporary basis to the highest bidder than by surrendering them gratis as tenth wife to some doddering old yam farmer. By adopting this philosophy, they hope that by the end of a short career involving the minimum of physical effort and no emotional entanglement whatsoever they will have saved enough to keep them in comparative luxury for the rest of their lives. Caroline,' continued the Reverend Father remorselessly as I tried in vain to stem this torrent of Irish nonsense, 'is one of those. Her charges, in case you are interested, are ten shillings per night for the straight stuff. If, however, you happen to be feeling particularly frisky and in the mood for something more exotic, it will cost you one West African pound a throw, including tax. Bush girls like Caroline prefer the orthodox stuff. They are girls of simple habits and they tend to become uncomfortable when asked to attempt new-fangled European divarications. They have a particular distaste for oral sex and sure, who can blame them? The view down there must be pretty horrible . . .'

'PADDY!' I exploded, 'For Christ's sake, SHUT UP!'

He leaned back in his chair and roared with laughter at my obvious discomfiture.

'I did not ask you for a lecture on the lifestyle of prostitutes,' I stated coldly. 'Anyway,' I continued suspiciously, 'you're supposed to be a priest. How did you get to know all this stuff?'

'We have our methods,' he replied mysteriously. Then he relented: 'The stories I get in African markets,' he said, 'are lessons on life in the raw that you will never be taught in the seminary. For news of what is happening in the real world, you cannot beat an old market mammy – she knows everything that's going on in every hole and corner of her community. It's good entertainment if you're prepared to listen. Besides,' he concluded virtuously, 'in what other way would you expect we poor old priests to get our kicks?'

I fixed him with a long and quizzical look. 'Paddy,' I said finally, 'at the back of all this rubbish you've been spouting, I sense a story. Tell me about Caroline.'

He stubbed out his cigarette and lifted his beer glass. His story was a sad one, and it was a story as old as humanity itself.

Caroline was the daughter of the local chief, an old illiterate cocoa farmer of great wealth and much influence in the area, whom Paddy had easily converted to Christianity soon after establishing his mission. She was very intelligent and had sailed through her early schooling with such high results that Paddy had, without difficulty, been able to get her a grant from his Bishop to go for further education in the distant city of Lagos.

A bush girl from the Iteru swamps simply had no chance among the city lights and the wide boys of Lagos. The money she should have spent on her education went on the purchase of pretty dresses and other folderols, so that, suddenly finding herself destitute, she turned to the oldest game in the world to recoup her losses.

In true African fashion, news of her fall from grace filtered back through the hundreds of miles of bush and swamp to her father. Mortified, the old man set off posthaste for the city and dragged her back ignominiously to her home.

The old man put her to work on his farm to keep her busy and out of mischief. It was not a success. She had been spoiled by her life in the city and she had little taste for any-thing resembling physical labour. Nor could her father always be around to watch her, and her good looks and easy virtue made her a target for every red-blooded male in Iteru. In desperation, her father approached his friend Paddy. Truth to tell, Paddy was sorely in need of someone to help out in his little school, someone intelligent and with a nat-ural affinity with children. Caroline would have suited perfectly. There was, however, a major stumbling block – Paddy had first to obtain permission from his Bishop, who lived at the diocese headquarters far upcountry. He, having heard of his protégé's downfall, was not nearly so forgiving as Paddy. He kept hedging . . . and hedging . . . and hedging.

And so it came about that, on the last Sunday of each month, the forlorn figure of Miss Caroline Ademugu could be seen trudging up the incline to the Iteru mission with the ever hopeful plea on her lips: 'Any news, Fadder?'

Three months had elapsed since I had last seen Paddy, and so busy had I been that I had thought about him only fleet-ingly, and of Caroline not at all. Now, here I was back on his verandah on a blazing hot Sunday, rumbles of thunder on the horizon signalling the approach of the rain season. A sunbird, carmine-chested, its head and throat glinting a metallic green in the harsh afternoon sun, gripped the slen-der stalk of a hibiscus flower on the bush by the verandah, its long, curved beak buried deep in the scarlet blossom. We chatted about this and that, and then I remembered my last visit.

'Whatever became of Caroline?' I asked. Paddy looked vaguely troubled. He had just begun to answer when an apologetic 'Excuse me, please,' came from the end of the verandah. There she was, looking, if possible, even more lovely than when I had last seen her. 'Any news yet, Fadder?' she asked, and her voice was filled with such pathos that I could not help but feel sorry for her.

'Well, Caroline,' replied Paddy slowly, 'I'm afraid that the news is bad. The Bishop has finally made up his mind and, because of your misbehaviour in Lagos, he will not agree for me to employ you.'

She stared at him for a few seconds in total disbelief. Then she sprang vertically in the air like a gazelle, fairly stamping her feet on the wooden floor of the verandah as she bounded up and down before us in a paroxysm of rage, screaming vituperations the while in her own language. At last she stopped, breathing heavily, sweat running down her face and her eyes burning with hatred. She fairly spat her parting words at Paddy:

'Fadder, you have wasted all my fucking time!'

The silence that followed her departure was finally broken by a long, deep sigh from my friend.

'What can one say but "yes" to that?' said the Reverend Father Patrick Sean O'Leary sadly.

6

Bani of the Graves

'**B**ani of the Graves', they called her. She was about seven years of age when we found each other, and she may have been all of eight years of age when I lost her. But her age doesn't matter. What matters is that I shall never forget her.

The forests of Siloni are just about the last places on earth you would expect to find one of the great loves of your life. They lie deep inside Africa's rainforest region and, in my day, they were dank and sombre places. Great, moss-covered brimstone trees crowded shoulder to shoulder with the mighty red ironwoods where they burst into leaf far up there at the roof of the world, turning day into permanent twilight for all of we forest residents. Here and there, where some ancient forest monarch had served its time on earth and come thundering down in a tangle of liane, the burning sun of Africa would, for the brief period of the dry season, be permitted to shed its light on the forest floor. But such moments of light amidst the darkness were few and far between; holes created in the canopy by such natural causes would fill up again with astonishing rapidity, so profuse was the vegetal fecundity of this part of the rainforest. Only by the river that cut its way through these funereal forests could one expect to find sunshine reaching the woodland floor with reasonable certainty on any given day, and even then the river was far too narrow for most of its length to allow more than the occasional fitful shaft of light to penetrate. It was where the river widened out into large pools on the approach to a fall or a gradient that one could bask in the sun's warmth, and it was at one such pool that the villagers of Siloni drew their water, performed their daily ablutions, and threw their castnets in the relative cool of the evening when the crayfish and the freshwater crabs came out from under the shelter of the stones on the river bottom to cluster in the shallows.

Once a month or so during the dry season a white Catholic Father would travel over the long and terrible track from the outside world to preach in the tiny, mud-walled church on the village outskirts. He made no secret of his dislike of this dreary place and, while it was usually necessary for him to sleep the night in the little church after his duties were over, the sun would no sooner have climbed over the forest tops the following morning than he would putter off back up the laterite trail to his mission in the distant city as fast as the wheels of his motor-scooter would carry him.

But the brevity of his visits meant that only the converted (or – perhaps more correctly for this remote part where the gods of the forest would always claim a higher place in the pantheon than any Christian god – the pseudo-converted) would have any real contact with this white man, and they were few. Most of the inhabitants were pagan to a man and proud of it, and to them he was but a vassal of the White Man's god sent to seduce them from their multifarious deities with silver words. The women and children were frankly terrified of him, for he was huge and bearded, with a booming voice and black satanic eyes, and they would hide in their huts until he had gone.

There had been a time, though, when white men had been a much more common sight around those parts. But that was long ago. At the turn of the century there had been, briefly, a sizable German trading post here. Wild rubber had been in abundance in the surrounding forests and, in those days, there were plenty of rainforest leopard. Unlike its more pallid cousin of the East African plains, the forest leopard had a coat of the richest old-gold hue, and this commanded the highest of prices in the markets of Europe. The fierce little forest elephants were to be found here, too, and their tusks, though small, contained ivory that was the hardest and whitest of all. Add to this the steady trickle of gold to be panned from the river, and this particular trading post had been one that looked to have a bright future.

Mother Africa, inevitably, put paid to that optimism. 'Take care and beware the Bight of Benin; there's ten comes out for forty goes in,' has always held true for the 'White Man's Grave'. Within the space of a dozen terrible days the whole of the German community had been wiped out by yellow fever, and within two short years the jungle had reclaimed the trading station. It had never been reopened.

It was to be another half century before any white man other than the priest ventured into those sombre forests again. In the early 1950s I arrived with a small crew of men to do a river survey. The chief gave me a room in his hut for my own use and a couple of other huts for my workers. When I had seen the men comfortably settled and had completed the obligatory introductory courtesies with the chief, I took my towel and a bar of soap down the hill to the river.

As was the custom with most tribes, men and women had their own separate bathing points around the pool. The chief had his own private section, and he had granted me permission to use this for the duration of my stay. It was a charming little nook surrounded by thick bushes, and the dappled sunshine sparkled on water that was deep and cool-looking and inviting. A small ramp of sticks had been built from the bank so that one could dry oneself without getting one's feet dirty. Several times I fancied I heard rustling sounds in the bushes and once I thought I saw the merest glimmer of a blur of movement beyond the wall of green. I carried on with my bathing, at the same time keeping a careful watch out of the corner of my eye. Finally, I was satisfied that my senses had not been playing tricks on me.

'Why were the village girls spying on me down at the pool?' I asked the old chief abruptly when I got back to the hut. He looked momentarily disconcerted, then he laughed out loud. 'I followed them down the hill and caught them at it,' he said. 'They told me that they had never seen a white man naked, and they wondered whether you were white all over, or whether your important bits were black like all normal men!'

He took me to the German graves the following morning. They were eighteen in number, each marked by a badly eroded concrete headstone. Much of the lettering on them was illegible, but from what I could make out the victims had all appeared to be in their early twenties when they died.

The little plot of land in which they lay was obviously being well cared for. The grass and creeping vines had been newly cut and an ancient hibiscus flowered in scarlet profusion at the far end. 'The Catholic Father pays me five pounds every year to keep it clean,' explained the chief, 'and I employ one of the village children to look after it. She sleeps under that bush mostly' – he pointed to a luxuriantly beautiful yellow-flowering erythrina shrub growing up the hill at the top end of the plot – 'for she is crazy and so has no one to take proper care of her.'

My ablutions that evening attracted even greater attention. The girls had become bolder, and I got the occasional glimpse of a brown face peeking out from behind a tree or a bush and distinct sounds of suppressed giggling. One cheeky young monkey was even so frisky as to unwrap her loincloth, expose herself momentarily to me and wave before vanishing again into the shadows. But I had become resigned to the fact that I would be the focus of attention for a day or two until the novelty wore off, so I decided to ignore them.

I was stepping out of the water and reaching for my towel when the hullabaloo began. The surrounding bushes exploded into an uproar of screams and shouts and the sounds of physical mayhem. I dropped my towel instantly and dived into the undergrowth, thinking that one of them must have stepped on a gaboon viper or a green mamba – both common in this area. I pulled up sharply. On the ground, fighting and clawing and swearing luridly while she was being kicked around by about half a dozen lusty teenage girls, was a little girl of about seven years of age.

I think, on reflection, that her assailants could not have been more alarmed by the appearance of a venomous serpent in their midst than by a stark naked white man, and they disappeared in the twinkling of an eye into the forest. The child appeared less bothered, but then I was to learn later that she took just about everything in life in her stride. She picked herself up and followed me back to where my clothes lay. While I was getting dressed, she told me her story.

Her name was Bani of the Graves. She was an orphan, her parents having been killed some years previously by a buffalo. She had no friends, because everyone said she was insane. The villagers would have driven her away into the forest to die long ago but for the fact that the chief had taken pity on her. Also, the witchdoctor had seen a vision on the night her parents had died that told him that, should any harm befall her, evil would befall the village. The chief's wives fed her whatever scraps were going, she said, and she it was who tended the 'White Graves' up on the hill.

She had a sad little old-young face with great big liquescent eyes, and her skin was of a light-chocolate hue. She was as thin as a stick insect. She spoke a quaint sort of Old World English sprinkled with expressions that – I was to find out later – she had picked up while listening to the occasional peripatetic African rubber trader who came into the area from the outside world to barter with the chief. No doubt picked up from the same source, she had a rich command of colourful invective.

'Why were those girls beating you?' I queried.

Because, she informed me, she had seen the girls watching me and she had considered it rude of them to do so to a guest of the village while he was bathing. They had taken exception to the rather peremptory way in which she had told them to go away.

We became instant friends. Although she had never spoken to a white man before that day, she attached herself to me like a limpet. She showed me the lean-to under the erythrina tree where she slept most nights through the dry season. It was a crude construction of sections of bark lashed to poles with pieces of liane. A rolled-up sleeping mat stood on its end in one corner and a little stick table occupied the other corner. A flat stone holding a large lump of agba tree resin for lighting purposes stood on the centre of the table, and a few unidentifiable knick-knacks were scattered around it. Seldom had I seen more spartan human accommodation anywhere. Only the golden glow of the erythrina blossoms and the kaleidoscopic shimmer of a tiny sunbird flitting among them above our heads afforded some relief from the heart-tugging starkness of this little girl's existence.

'Are you not afraid to be by yourself?' I asked curiously, knowing from experience the inherent dread most bush Africans had for places of the dead and the evil spirits that haunted them by night. 'No,' she replied simply. 'For it is well known that mad people are not afraid of anything.'

The old chief knew her better than any. He told me that, although she often slept just inside the door of his hut while the rains were at their most intense, she refused to stay with any of his wives. Indeed, he confided, no one really wanted her because she was not as other children were. She never played with the others, and she never even occupied herself with the solitary games that other African children played when left to their own devices.

She was as self-sufficient as any woman, and the village women were more than a little afraid of her, saying that she had been old when she was born. They were afraid of her for many reasons, not the least of them being because she had strange dreams, ridiculous dreams. She dreamed that the stars in the heavens were other worlds and she dreamed of huge silver houses coming down to earth from them in showers of moondust. She dreamed of worlds that were completely white and so cold that nothing could live in them, and she dreamed that once it had been so in Africa, too. She dreamed of monstrous lizards as tall as trees and more fearsome than the leopard that had lived here when the earth was young. She dreamed of many such things, said the chief, and everyone knew that these were the dreams of the mentally unstable.

But she was a child and she was harmless, so he humoured her. He was amused at the way in which she had so obviously and so instantly taken to me, so, when a few weeks after my arrival I told him that I had to move further upriver for a fortnight with my crew to continue my survey, he offered no objection when Bani of the Graves stated firmly that she was going along too to 'take care' of me. Although he was too polite to say so, I could see by his demeanour that he was thinking 'to each his own', or whatever was the tribal equivalent.

In truth, the last thing I needed when setting off on a camping expedition in the wilds of Africa for a couple of weeks was a small child, particularly one who – by her own admission – was eccentric, to say the least. But she was so confident, yet so *alone*, that I hadn't the heart to refuse her.

I need not have worried. She was of immense help. She clucked after me like a mother hen taking care of a solitary chick. African children are taught from a very early age how to look after others, but this one was something special. She kept my tent spick-and-span, and she washed my clothes at the riverside while we were all away at work in the forest, draping the garments over the rocks in the patches of sunlight to dry. 'If you hang them on bushes, you'll get ticks,' she cautioned. She proved – at least, insofar as I was concerned – to be a snob of the highest order, for she would not let me eat with the workers. She cooked for me while we were working, often shamelessly filching from the workers' store of dried fish or monkey meat or whatever they had stashed away for themselves to cook on their return from the forest. I shared my food with her, of course, but she refused to eat until I had finished, saying that it was not seemly for a woman to be seen eating in the presence of men.

The workers teased her mercilessly, pretending to steal my clothing while it was drying down by the river. Two of her favourite words were 'scram' and 'bastard', and at such times she would stand between them and my clothes, her tiny figure quivering with fury as she raged at them: 'Scram, you bastards, scram!' Twice I returned home from work a little later than usual, with the workers all already in camp, to find her waiting outside my tent, her face like thunder, greeting me with the words: 'These bastards have been at it again, Papa!'

She slept on the mat just inside my tent, and woe betide the intruder who might have been so brave or so foolish as to try to enter my tent in the still watches of the night while Bani of the Graves was keeping vigil over me.

When the rain and the mists had gone from the forest, the river could be as attractive as any Highland river. Its clear, shallow waters meandered sleepily over stony beds and around small moraines of smooth, mossy boulders. Great ropes of liane trailed from on high all the way down to the water, and weirdly shaped trees formed an umbrella over it for much of the way, with deep pools forming at intervals below this umbrella. The caterpillars and other insects that rained down constantly from the overhanging branches fed an assortment of catfish, perch and tigerfish in those pools, and, as I brought a cheap old spinning rod with me, what better way to while away a lazy Sunday afternoon than by loafing by the riverside?

Bani of the Graves came with me. 'White Man's Fishing', as she called it, fascinated her. I made her a tiny rod of bamboo cane, affixing a length of nylon and a hook to it and baiting it with a juicy caterpillar or whatever else came to hand. She even hooked a half-pound perch with this outfit on her first expedition with me and her excitement was intense.

To the casual observer it might have been reminiscent of a scene from a Mark Twain story as we sat on the river bank, chatting and laughing, white man and scrawny little black girl side by side. Sometimes I would let her hold my spinning rod, but it was much too big and cumbersome for her. Nevertheless she took enormous pride in the fact that I allowed her to do so and she would always try to make sure she was holding it whenever any of the workers were in the vicinity. 'Those bastards aren't civilized, Papa,' she would remark with satisfaction as we watched the crew wending their way upriver with their crude fish traps and their primitive spears.

The time went past all too quickly. On our last day, while the workers were packing up the gear in readiness for the trip out, she was unusually quiet and withdrawn. That night she did something she had never done before: at one point I woke with a start, aware that the blanket around me was being raised ever so cautiously. I lay still, pretending to be asleep, and the tiny body huddled in close to my back. She was shivering ceaselessly, as though in an ague. 'A touch of fever,' I thought drowsily before I drifted off to sleep.

We returned to the village. On the following morning, as we were about to depart I saw her standing forlornly on her own at the edge of the crowd. I went over to her and picked her up. Teardrops, like liquid pearls on brown satin, ran down her cheeks. I promised her I'd come back to her with a brand-new 'White Man's Rod', junior-size, specially for her. 'Come back soon, Papa,' she whispered. 'Soon, I beg you. I am afraid. On our last night in bush, the stars were calling for me.'

A month later I stood on the main road at the junction of the twenty miles of track leading to the village. There was a barrier across the track guarded by armed police. The commander told me that following the death of the village chief the previous week fierce fighting had broken out between two rival factions. No one knew the cause of it, but all access to the village was temporarily forbidden. By the time I was allowed in, the village was deserted. Of Bani of the Graves, there was no sign.

It was to be a further year before I was able to return to the area for one final visit. I was carrying with me her 'White Man's Rod', still in its shiny bright blue plastic casing, hoping against hope. Some of the huts had been occupied again, but the inhabitants were all strangers to me. The graveyard was unkempt, already beginning its return to the jungle, and her little lean-to had collapsed inward and over her pathetic few possessions.

I ran into a hunter who claimed to remember me from my last visit. He made reassuring noises. 'Maybe the women killed her when the chief died,' he said vaguely, 'for they were afraid of her and they hated her. But then again, maybe she just ran away into the forest to live with the animals. She was mad, you know.'

Even faint hope is better than no hope. I hung around the area for another week, searching the surrounding forest. But I knew it was no use. I knew in my heart of hearts that Bani of the Graves had gone from this world and that the witchdoctor's prophecy had come true. She had said she was going to marry me when she was old enough, you see, and in Africa such things are not said lightly. Especially if you are seven years of age and quite mad like Bani of the Graves. Had she been alive she would have known I was there and she would have come to find me.

I laid the rod in its pretty blue wrapper on the carpet of fallen flowers under the erythrina bush. It will still be there, should the more adventurous among you find yourselves in the dark, wet forests of Siloni.

But you would do well to keep your hands off it. Bani of the Graves will be around there, too, in spirit. Somewhere. You can be sure of that. Among the great orchid-covered boughs of the towering brimstone trees, perhaps, or by the side of the chuckling waters where we used to sit, or in the drumming of the rain on the red forest path where we used to walk. And certainly she will be there with the glory of the sunbird in the fragrant yellow blossoms above the ruins of her earthly abode.

She will be there, taking care of the things that were precious to her. Taking care of me, too, for my spirit is there along with her.

And don't any of you bastards ever forget it.

7

Visiting Aunt Matilda

'**W**hen ye get ower tae Canada,' instructed my Great-Aunt Teen, 'be sure and visit my sister Matilda. She'll be pleased tae see ye.'

I was very fond of old Teen. A spinster with a sharp sense of humour, she had lived in Perthshire all her life and she owned a raspberry farm on the outskirts of Blairgowrie. I did not see her often, especially now that I was working overseas, but I would never have dreamed of passing by her way without paying a visit and even spending the occasional night at her place. On this occasion, I was home on leave from Africa. Sitting by her fire one bleak November night, I made some incautious remark about my ambition to visit Canada one day.

'Whereabouts in Canada,' I enquired, 'does your sister Matilda live?'

'A place called Sidney, on Vancouver Island,' replied

she. 'Ye take the boat from Vancouver to Victoria. When ye reach Victoria, ask for her. She says everybody kens her there, for that's where she does maist o' her shopping.'

My dear old Aunt Teen had never been out of Scotland in her life, so far as I was aware. The vastness of a country like Canada would have been quite beyond her scope of understanding. I said gently: 'I think you'll have to give me a wee bit more information than that, Aunt Teen, just in case.' She hunted around in her sideboard, fished out an old letter, and handed it to me. 'Ye'll find her address on that,' she said. I tucked the envelope carefully into my wallet.

'I havenae seen her in years,' said Aunt Teen sadly, 'but I've telt her all aboot ye. She'll make ye awfie welcome whenever ye get there.' She brought the bottle over and poured me a good stiff dram. 'Ye'll have nae bother finding her,' she continued. 'She says they all call her Auntie Matilda in Sidney.'

I lifted the glass up level with my eyes. The flickering firelight danced in delicate prismatic shades of colour on the crystal, and the amber liquor looked warm and comforting as the cold winter blast rattled the eaves outside.

It was, in fact, to be some years later before I was to find myself en route to Canada. I had a month at my disposal and a leisurely spell of drifting here and there around the Rockies seemed as good a way of passing the time as any. Besides, it would give me a chance of fulfilling my long-standing promise to Aunt Teen.

Calgary, that oil and rodeo city on the edge of the great prairies, was my first port of call. I have never been fond of cities of any kind, especially busy industrial cities, but

Calgary had the advantage of being on the fringe of the Rockies and thus conveniently enough sited for me to be able to rest up for a day or two and figure out which direction out of it I should take. The direct rail or road line to Vancouver would have been the obvious route, but I was in no great rush to see Aunt Matilda, particularly as I had told no one, even Aunt Teen, that I was in Canada. Aunt Matilda would enjoy the surprise, I figured, and besides, I wanted to do a bit of exploring before getting bogged down with elderly relatives. The name 'Calgary', too, had always fascinated me, for this bustling city of some three-quarters of a million people had been named, incredibly, after the tiniest of Scottish communities, Calgary on the Isle of Mull, home of my forebears. The name itself came from the Gaelic *Cala a' gharaidh*, or haven by the wall.

It was in a bar in Calgary that I heard of a remarkable character who had a homestead some sixty miles to the north-west. Old Nell, as she was now called, had left Galloway in Scotland when she was eighteen years of age to settle in Canada shortly after the turn of the twentieth century. She had never returned to her native land. She had quickly adapted to the pioneering life, and long after the Old West had succumbed to the New had remained a complete anachronism. Even as late as the 1940s a familiar sight on the dirt road approaching Calgary had been Nell perched high on her buckboard, ki-yipping at the pitch of her voice and whip cracking like pistol shots as the team forded the shallows of the Bow River, water spraying in all directions from the flying hooves as her horses thundered towards town for the monthly supplies for the homestead. She was still very much alive, my informant told me, though no longer to be seen with buckboard and horses. She still stayed on at the farm, even though she had been on her own for a few years now since her husband died and her family had gone. Pretty spry for an eighty-something-year-old, he said, and he was sure she would be glad to have someone from the Old Country visit her.

I left the following morning. I located her homestead easily, for everyone knew her. The cabin was quite some distance in from the road and in the most picturesque of locations. A forest of graceful evergreens stood tall and straight behind it, with clumps of deciduous trees and shrubs scattered higgledy-piggledy among them. Beyond were the blue masses of the Rockies, a picture-postcard scene glowing in the morning sun.

The cabin was large and typically Canadian, with a roof of shingles. A figure in faded blue overalls was astraddle the rooftop, its back to me. I cupped my hands to my mouth and shouted, 'HELLO!' and it turned round to peer at me. To my astonishment, I saw that it was an elderly lady. 'Wait a meenit,' she called down in the thickest of Scottish brogues. 'I'm comin' doon.' She stood up, and walking with the confidence of a tightrope walker she made her way to the end of the roof where the ladder was propped.

She stood before me. She was short in stature and thin and wiry of body. Her face was the face of an outdoors woman, the face of one who had seen the sun and the wind and the rain and the blizzards of many a Canadian season. But her eyes were the eyes of a young girl, clear and sparkling as the mountain streams in her native land. They were the eyes of a woman in love with life. I told her who I was and where I was from and we just stood looking in silence at each other for a moment or two. Then 'Come awa' in,' she said, 'and we'll get the kettle on.'

Like Nell herself, the living room was neat and clean and cheerful. Family photographs lined the walls and the mantelpiece. Over tea she told me about her late husband and her family, now scattered far and wide in a variety of occupations. She had never lost her accent, she told me proudly, for she had never felt any need to discard it. Those who pretended not to understand her were not worth knowing anyway. 'Besides,' she pointed out, 'Canada was founded on guid plain Scotch.'

I did not dare ask her what business an eighty-something old lady had scrambling over the roof of a house repairing shingles. Instead I asked her about her horses. She no longer had horses, she said, 'because some folk cannae be trusted these days'. 'Rustlers,' she replied shortly, when I raised an enquiring eyebrow.

'Rustlers?' I exclaimed in disbelief, for I had thought that that sort of activity had died out with the demise of the James brothers.

'Aye, rustlers,' she repeated.

It transpired that, some ten years previously, while Nell still had her team of horses, the magnificent white stallion that had been the lead horse had vanished one night. Neither the local police nor the Mounties had been able to find any trace of it, but Nell had her suspicions. She paid a visit to a remote homestead. There she found her stallion, alive and well but dyed a fetching black hue. Nell had come prepared, and only the arrival of the police and a posse of neighbours had saved the culprit from the father and mother of all thrashings from the horsewhip she had brought along.

She took me on a tour of her property. At one time, when her husband had been able to manage it, parts of it had been under the plough. Nell didn't bother any more and now it was all reverting to its natural state. She preferred it that way, anyway, she said. She loved wild creatures and she liked them to be able to roam free and unmolested over her land. Snowshoe hares were abundant, covered in long brown hair at this time of the year but a pristine white when the snows of winter arrived. The woodchuck was common in the open spaces, dining on the plentiful supply of lush green grass, and the mule deer, she said, came down from the foothills in the winter. Often at that time of the year when she drew back the curtains of the window in the morning she would see them gathered in small groups all round the house, trampling down the snow to expose the grass and the lichens underneath. Porcupines caused a wee bit of damage to the young trees by gnawing at the bark, she said, but ach, there were plenty of trees around, anyway.

Later that morning we walked round her property. There were, indeed, plenty of trees around, growing naturally as all trees are meant to do. Tall jack pine, Douglas fir, white spruce and western red cedar were dominant, but plenty of the white boles of birch and aspen were mingled among them. I remarked that, because of neglect and overcrowding some of the smaller spruce and cedar were looking a bit sickly. 'Weel, you're the forester,' she retorted. 'What should be done aboot them?'

'Only one thing to do,' I replied. 'Remove them. With someone who knows what he's doing, it shouldn't take more than a week.'

'Good!' she said firmly. 'That's it settled then. Aunt Matilda can wait. You and me can stert on them the morn, and ye can pit up in my spare bedroom for the week!'

I tried to think up some plausible excuse, but one glance at this feisty old lady beside me told me that it would be a waste of time. 'Okay,' I said meekly.

We came across some curious pipes sticking out of the ground. Nell told me that some months previously a large oil company based in Calgary had made sample drillings on her property. The results must have interested them very much, for each week since then various important-looking officials had been arriving at her place with offers for her property, each offer being very substantially larger than the previous one. The last offer, she said, had been accompanied by a vague threat as to how unpleasant the consequences could be should she continue to refuse to put pen to paper.

'What did you say to them?' I asked.

'Nothin' jist then,' she said. 'I jist turned my back on them and went intae the hoose, got the auld Winchester, loaded it up in front of them, and telt them they had three seconds tae get back intae their cars and bugger off doon the road before I started shootin'.'

'And did they bugger off?'

'They shit themselves,' she said with obvious satisfaction. 'Ye couldnae see their cars for dust.'

The only woodcutting tools of any kind Nell had were an axe and a bowsaw, but they sufficed. None of the trees we would be felling were of large diameter. We worked steadily in her woods the whole week and the sights and smells around us gave us huge appetites. Red squirrels scampered in the treetops, flycatchers and robins were everywhere, and the skies were the bluest blue you ever saw in your life. In her own forthright fashion, Nell said that it was the most fun she had ever had without taking her clothes off. As for me, I had never known time moving so fast.

We parted without any fuss, without any ostentatious displays of affection, as true friends should be able to do. A neighbouring farmer had offered to give me a lift to Edmonton, where I would be able to catch a westbound train through the Rockies. As I was about to climb into the truck, Old Nell squeezed my hand.

'Regards tae Aunt Matilda,' she whispered.

I stopped off at the little town of Houston, on the main road halfway between Prince George and Prince Rupert, for no other reason than that I was bored with travelling and felt like resting up for a few days. The town did not inspire me, but a nearby saloon did. The only other customer was Frenchie, and in no time at all we were chatting as though we had known each other all our lives.

Frenchie was swarthy, lean and hungry-looking, a man of uncertain middle age. He was the product of a drunken Québécois trapper and a Palestinian lady of the night. It had been a somewhat volatile marriage, and Frenchie had been left to look after himself at a very early age. Liver failure had taken his father, and his mother had vanished into the obscurity from whence she had originated.

From the beginning he had been a jack-of-all-trades. Currently unemployed, he had at one time or another been a trapper, gold panner, tourist guide, long-distance lorry driver, logger, a totem pole carver . . . The best job he had ever had in his life, he told me wistfully, had been his employment by a wealthy American lady who had used Vancouver as a base for touring the Rockies and communing with nature in the raw. As it turned out, the only nature in the raw she had communed with during her two months holed up in the most luxurious hotel in Vancouver had been

Frenchie, who had been a kitchen scullion when she arrived and her gigolo two days later. He had convinced her that he was a full-blooded Apache chief, a scandalous confidence trick, for Frenchie, apart from not having a drop of Indian blood in his veins, was well aware that there was not a single Apache, full-blooded or otherwise, within a hundred square miles of where he was having his evil way with her.

But the information had seemed to add zip to her passion, he said, and the money had been good. She had a Pomeranian dog that was just as pampered as its mistress and that she insisted should be allowed to lie at the foot of their bed. It would gurr discontentedly, he said, if the turbulence between the sheets became too boisterous for its liking. She had brought with her its personal gold plate from which it was fed twice daily on the choicest fillet steaks, and the hotel management had to ensure that it had a constant supply of mineral water in a silver bowl in the room. On the day on which they parted, never to meet again, he had purloined the silver bowl as a memento. 'And,' he added, 'I kicked the dog's ass for good measure.'

He suggested a fishing trip to the forests surrounding the little community of Noralee, some distance to the southeast. The area was full of steelheads, he said. I had heard of the steelhead, but had never seen one. I knew it to have a reputation of being a highly contentious variety of rainbow trout – indeed, most ichthyologists made no distinction between the two, and the only difference between them would appear to have been that the steelhead was a rainbow that migrated to the sea at some point in its life before returning to the rivers and streams years later to spawn. Their different style of feeding in the sea made them tastier – and larger – than ordinary rainbow trout. In the area to which he proposed to take me, said Frenchie, they commonly exceeded ten pounds in weight.

We would be camping out. Frenchie had friends in the village and we were able to hire all the necessary equipment and fishing gear, and we also bought some basic food supplies.

The weather stayed fine and the fishing was superb. The handsome steelheads, a shining grey-brown of back, with dark chocolate brown speckles and daffodil-yellow bellies, practically fought each other for the privilege of being hooked by us. We kept only the best. Each morning a couple of taciturn old men would be waiting by our bivouacs to take our surplus catch back with them. 'They smoke them and sell them,' explained Frenchie, 'and it guarantees me free board and lodgings any time I'm in the area.'

Those wild woods were full of life. Tracks of moose were seen but we never came across any. We did spy a pair of river otters, though, just as darkness was falling one evening. They were loping along on the bank of a stream, one behind the other, when they spotted us. They stood up on their hind legs for the briefest of moments to get a better look, then they slipped silently into the water. Frenchie told me that they had been known to bore holes in beaver dams to drain the water so that they could feast on the fish and frogs stranded as a result.

Throughout the day the great grey owl ghosted its way through the trees in its never-ending quest for voles. For such a large bird it was the most silent living thing I had ever known in flight and the first time it skimmed out past my head in the gloom of an evening I nearly gave birth. Its anonymous grey coloration made it practically impossible to see when it was perched and still, but whenever I did manage to see one at such times it was always sitting bolt upright, neck stretched and golden eyes wide and alert, a sort of disapproving look on its face that reminded me irresistibly of some fuddy-duddy Victorian alderman who had just been told an obscene story at the Lord Mayor's Banquet.

My nights were spent sitting by the fire drinking black coffee and listening to Frenchie's incredible yarns. His colourful life had made him an absolute treasure trove of reminiscences. There was peace in those remote woods, and one felt completely removed from all the woes of humanity within them. The only slight inconvenience during the whole of my time there was in having been so careless as to have lost a rather splendid and expensive wristwatch that I had purchased in London in a moment of extravagance some six weeks previously. A search up and down the river bank on which we had been fishing had failed to reveal any trace of it and I had regretfully had to accept the fact that it must have dropped in the water.

At the end of our tenth day Frenchie had gone to bed early, saying he was tired. He had been unusually quiet all day and I had mostly left him alone with his thoughts. I sat by the fire for a time in the darkness, throwing in the odd bit of stick to keep it going, staring into the glowing red of the embers and the flickering yellow of the flames, thinking about nothing much at all. Finally, I dowsed the fire and went off to my sleeping quarters.

I was up at the usual time the following morning. A heavy mist filtered through the trees, making the air of morning damp and chilly. I glanced upstream and froze. Frenchie had gone. His bivouac had vanished, and not a trace of him remained.

I lit a fire and made myself some coffee while I figured

out what I should do. I knew I could easily find my way back to the village, but this sudden exodus was nevertheless a shock to the system.

I was on my second coffee when a figure came walking down the stream bank towards me. I recognized him as being one of the men who had been picking up the fish from us. He squatted down in front of me and I poured him a coffee. 'Where's Frenchie?' I asked. He remained silent, just squatting there sipping at his coffee, his eyes fixed on mine. When eventually he spoke, it was to answer me indirectly, in an oblique way: 'Frenchie is a man for himself. He has always gone his own way, like the grey owl. He has always stayed just one jump ahead of the law. Yesterday morning, when we came to collect the fish, we came with news for him. We warned him that someone was looking for him. He had to go. It would have been dangerous for him to stay.'

'What sort of warning? Who was looking for him? What's he done? Where's he gone?' The words tumbled out of me.

The man before me shrugged his shoulders, not replying, his face and his eyes expressionless. I knew then that I would never know the answers to my questions. Suddenly I felt that it would be better for me not to know.

He said, 'I'll help you get your gear out to the main road, and you can get transport up the Prince Rupert road from there.'

He stood up and began to gather up the pots and pans while I attended to my tent and sleeping equipment. As we were about to head out, he turned to me. He put his hand in his pocket and said, 'Frenchie said to give this back to you. And he tole me to tell you "sorry".'

In the palm of his hand he had my watch.

If someone were to ask me what has been the most spectacularly beautiful sea trip I have ever been on, I should not
even have to think twice. I cannot believe that there is a
more picturesque one anywhere in the world than the fairy-
tale ferry trip from Prince Rupert via the Inside Passage to
Port Hardy on Vancouver Island.

I was, at last, on my way to see Aunt Matilda. It had
taken me a lot longer than I had initially planned, but then
there had been interesting diversions on the way. Like
Thoreau, I have always tended to walk to the beat of a different drummer, and perhaps the mañana style of life I had
become so accustomed to in the African rainforests had not
done much to civilize me. Since leaving Frenchie and whatever problem he had, I had spent a week of doing very little
in the Hazelton area and a couple of days pottering around
the scenic port of Prince Rupert. Now, I had the tang of the
sea in my face with a vengeance, and in another fifteen or
sixteen hours I would be on Vancouver Island.

The beauty around me was extraordinary. Rugged
fjords and montane forest stretched in an unbroken line
north to south all the way down the coast to the left of us
while, to the right, a necklace of islands, equally thickly
wooded, acted as a buffer against the fierce Pacific storms.

The passage was narrow, and small towns and fishing
communities were dotted here and there along both sides.
Bald eagles were much in evidence, diving swiftly down
from on high to the sea, sometimes even partly submerging
themselves, to rise cumbersomely with heavy flapping of
great wings, almost always with a large silvery fish in their
talons. In the Milbanke Sound, about halfway through our

voyage, we were briefly exposed to the open Pacific. But the sea was calm and we were treated to the magnificent spectacle of colossal humpback whales hurling themselves bodily out of the water to fall back with an almighty splash. God alone knew why they performed those acrobatics, for there seemed to be no useful purpose to them. The mischievous thought passed through my mind that it might have been a Canadian tourist gimmick organized by the then Premier, the colourful and indefatigable John G. Diefenbaker.

Fort Hardy had been named after Vice Admiral Sir Thomas Masterman Hardy, of Nelson and Trafalgar fame. It is a very small town whose economy was based, at least at the time of my visit, on copper mining, logging and fishing. In fact, logging and fishing were the mainstays of the whole of Vancouver Island then. It was in a Port Hardy coffee shop that I met Sven, a great hulking Swede who was employed as a logger further down the coast. He had been enjoying a weekend with some elderly friends in Port Hardy, he told me, and after he had gathered together some supplies he would be heading back to his camp.

'What are you doing here?' he asked with no great curiosity. 'Touristing?' 'Kind of,' I said. 'But now I'm on my way to visit my Aunt Matilda in Sidney at the other end of the island.'

I happily accepted his offer to carry me halfway down the island in his truck. At midday we met as prearranged at a bar in town. Sven had accumulated a considerable thirst since we had parted, and his first pint vanished in no time at all. I made no effort to keep up with him.

Swedes are supremely generous people. If they have a fault, it is that they won't take 'no' for an answer. They take

grave exception – especially when they have had a few
drinks – to having their offers of hospitality spurned. By the
time we got into his truck much, much later that afternoon,
I had committed myself to spending the night at his logging
camp. 'It won't hurt your old Auntie Matilda to wait for
another night,' he reasoned, 'especially as she has no idea
you are coming, anyway.'

Vancouver Island is about two hundred miles long. We
drove through lovely little coastal communities with names
like Alert Cove and Fanny Bay before turning off on to a
well-maintained logging road. Stands of colossal Douglas
firs lined the roadsides and their balsam-like fragrance
wafted headily through the open windows of the truck.

I knew I was in trouble the moment we entered the
saloon. Great hairy loggers crowded the premises from wall
to wall. It was nine o'clock at night, and it was obvious that
all were in fine fettle. My sports jacket and flannels drew
instant ribald commentary, and Sven's information that I
was on my way to visit my Auntie Matilda brought the
house down, for some reason not immediately apparent to
me. All of them looked about seven feet tall and they were
built like grizzlies.

The interior of the saloon was like something out of a
western film. The floor was of rough wooden planking with
a thick layer of sawdust and wood chippings over it. A large
bronze object that I took at first to be a jardinière occupied
the corner of the wall behind me; closer inspection revealed
it to be a spittoon, and even closer inspection proved that it
had not been placed there merely for decorative purposes,
either. The actual bar was very long and constructed of
three-inch-thick log-length planks, rough on sides and
bottom but smooth as glass on top. Glasses full to the brim

slid rapidly up the bar from barman to consumer without a drop being spilt, and the contents slid just as rapidly down cavernous maws, equally without a drop being spilt.

To this day I do not know how I survived that night. My memories of it are hazy and disjointed: of noise, raucous laughter, the endless clinking of glasses, feet stomping on the wooden floor, of cacophonous singing. At some point during the night a burly Australian picked up on the Auntie Matilda theme and began to sing: 'Auntie Matilda, Auntie Matilda, who'll come to Auntie Matilda with me . . .?' – a refrain that was elaborated upon with the anticipated vulgarity by the choristers. I paid not one cent over the bar in the whole of that night, for I was not allowed to do so. There seemed, indeed, to be a concerted effort by all present to float me down the road to Sidney on a tidal wave of all that was best – or worst – in Canadian alcohol, and when that damned barman dug out of his private stock a couple of large bottles of best Scotch malt whisky, opened them both and threw the corks away, I came very close to weeping tears of self-pity.

I woke late the following morning. I did not feel good at all, and I did not feel a whole lot better when I staggered through to the cookhouse in search of strong coffee or something lethal to end it all and the cook asked me if it was three or four fried eggs that I wanted for breakfast with my fatback pork, and did I like my eggs sunny-side up and with plenty of maple syrup poured over them? But the good news he had for me was that he was taking the truck to Victoria for supplies, and he could give me a ride there if I wished. He was leaving in an hour's time, so if I really didn't want breakfast . . .?

I was at long last on the final stage of my trip. One

night with Aunt Matilda and then I'd have to get back to Calgary. I wasted no time in Victoria other than to buy an armful of flowers for Aunt Matilda and then I tumbled into a cab.

I had no difficulty in finding the address. The problem was that no one seemed to be at home. 'Out shopping, maybe,' I mused. I decided to sit on her doorstep and await her arrival.

An elderly man emerged from the house next door. 'Are you looking for Auntie Matilda?' he enquired. When I nodded in affirmation, he continued chattily, 'Gee, you just missed her. If you'd been here yesterday you'd have gotten her at home. But she's gone off to visit her sister in the Old Country. They hadn't seen each other in a long time, so she thought she'd take the chance to go over while the fares were cheap and she felt like it. I told her to go for it. You don't get any younger, and you don't never know what's in store for you round the corner.'

His keen old eyes were studying me as he talked, looking me up and down, obviously trying to figure out who and what I was. He went on, 'She said that her sister had written to say that one of her nephews was due back from Africa any time now, and she was real anxious to see him for she hadn't seen him since he was a little baby. She said it would be a real surprise for him when she turned up unexpectedly on his doorstep . . .'

'Is your wife still with you?' I interrupted.

'Yup,' he answered. 'Confined to a wheelchair, but we get about okay.'

I gave him the flowers. 'Tell her these are compliments of Auntie Matilda,' I said.

I strode off down the road. A cheeky little robin

followed me, hedge-hopping alongside me, tut-tut-tutting at me as he saw me off his property. I breathed in deeply as I walked, filling my lungs with the crisp, pure Canadian air. Already I could feel the poisons of the night before clearing from my system.

8

The Power of Prayer

'**N**o Religious Discussions and No Sectarian Songs' sternly advised the large notice above the bar of the Lanarkshire pub where I had stopped to have a quiet drink. The atmosphere could not have been quieter on this day: four old men playing dominoes at a table in the far corner and another drinking silently by himself on a stool at the end of the bar.

The barman was chatty. It had not been so quiet the previous Saturday evening, he informed me. The pub had been packed to capacity with regulars from the nearby Ravenscraig steel factory when half a dozen soccer fans entered. They were wearing the green and white scarves of the Glasgow Celtic Football Club and they were on their way home to the south of Scotland after watching their team's demolition of their great rivals, the Glasgow Rangers.

Rangers have always been strongly allied to the

Protestant religion, while Celtic's roots are firmly embedded in their Catholic past. The rivalry between the two has often been bitter.

It may have been that, as strangers to the area, the visitors were unaware that they were passing through a part of Scotland in which Protestants and Freemasonry held sway, and the sympathy of the local population for the concept of papal authority could not, therefore have been expected to be other than minimal. Or it may have been that, fuelled by much Guinness before leaving Glasgow earlier that evening, they simply did not care. Whichever, they had obviously decided that it would be a good idea to regale their assembled – and by now ominously silent – audience with a song. It turned out to be a very bad idea indeed. The resultant fracas had only been quelled with the combined muscle of a platoon of Lanarkshire's constabulary, with considerable otiose adjustments being effected in the interim to the general mise en scène of the publican's licensed premises.

'May I ask,' I enquired with some curiosity, 'the nature of the song that so offended your regulars?'

He glanced nervously sideways to ensure that none of the others were eavesdropping. Then he leaned across the bar and put his mouth to my ear. 'Danny Boy,' he whispered.

To the outside world it would undoubtedly have seemed odd that such a universally popular song could trigger a major riot. But this was an Irish melody, and one with Catholic connotations to boot. Nor was the cause of the visitors helped by the fact that one of their team stalwarts had been called Danny McGrain. Quite apart from all this, though, it is a sad fact that at time of writing anyone who sings a 'wrong type of song' in the 'wrong neighbourhood' in

Scotland's west-central belt is either imbued with a death-wish or very drunk indeed.

Sectarianism exists in parts of the world other than Scotland and Ireland, of course, but it sometimes seems to me that it is within those two countries today that it is to be heard at its most raucous and seen at its most vulgar. Politicians and religious leaders on both sides of the Great Divide spew out their bile at each other and at those of us who have the temerity to suggest that their narrow, hate-filled views are not what Christianity is all about. The Christian ethic of tolerance to all is very far from the minds of those Neanderthals when they step up on their blue or green soapboxes to preach to their followers.

I had a fortunate start to life. My parents were of the Protestant faith, but by no means rigid about it. My father's dislike of religious leaders of all creeds was absolute, and he would have travelled many a long and weary mile to avoid them. His encounters with them were therefore rare, and when they did occur they were usually uncomfortable meet-ings. He arrived home one evening, having had a most convivial session with his cronies in the village pub. A pow-erful distillery fragrance preceded him like some hellish miasma as he entered the house, wafting headily over us and the local minister sitting by the fireside drinking tea. Father stood in the doorway in disbelief, momentarily stunned into silence by the sight of the clergyman sitting in his favourite chair. Then 'Good God, it's you!' he exclaimed. 'Not quite,' remarked the Man of God with dry pulpit humour, 'but you're getting there.'

Occasionally my mother would drag we children down the road to the Millisle kirk on Sunday mornings. Catching us to prepare us for the ordeal was never easy, for it always

seemed to be such a colossal waste of a perfectly good morning, especially when the burn was in spate after the
overnight rain and full of trout just waiting to be caught. My
brother George and I, being the two oldest of the family,
were the favourite targets for her oppression. We would be
hosed down and forced, struggling and biting, into our
Sunday best before setting off with her on the half-mile walk
to the place of worship. With the hindsight of many years, I
know it now to have been an ordinary and rather pleasant-
looking country church from the outside, so the few
remaining memories I have of its interior are fragmentary
and tinted with the bias of childhood: the sepulchral
gloominess; the hardness of the bare wooden pews; the weak
rays of sunlight filtering through the stained glass windows,
seeking vainly to pierce the dust rising slowly in crystalline
motes towards the roof, like searchlights trying to penetrate
a thick Solway fog; and most of all, the dreary solemnity of
the service. You could smell age and decay and death there.
Just dare to laugh or sneeze in that place and – you knew
without being told – God would have descended from His
throne Up There posthaste to smite thee with His Thunder
and His Lightning.

Religion was an exercise in boredom for we children. I
can recall only one moment of light relief in all the time I
went to church during those childhood years, and that was
when my brother spotted a large brown rat emerging from a
hole in the wall near to him. Never one to be so selfish as to
keep a secret to himself, he tapped the lady next to him
with his forefinger and silently pointed out the rodent. She,
alas, turned out to be not all that fond of rats, and she gave
very audible proof of her dislike of them by emitting a shriek
so loud and so penetrating that the collective hearts of the

worshippers stopped beating for a moment or two and the colony of crows in the wood outside rose to the sky as one in a black swirling cloud of cacophonous protest.

Sectarian intolerance never entered our lives as children, for the simple reason that there were no other religious denominations anywhere near us. Wigtownshire had always been a predominantly Protestant county. But I am quite sure that had our cottage been surrounded by Muslims, Hindi, Mormons, or whatever, neither we nor our parents would have been in the slightest put out. When the first few Catholics arrived at our school as evacuees from the wartime bombings, we were much more interested in the fact that they were city slickers, coming from a completely unknown environment to we country bumpkins. My memory tells me that they quickly became part of our community, part of our way of life, part of us, with the minimum of hassle. The same hand of friendship and tolerance exists through most of Galloway today, an irony, perhaps, when one considers that Wigtownshire, Galloway's most westerly county, is but a short hop across the water from the sectarian brutality and religious bigotry with which the Northern Ireland of today is sadly suffused.

The main Christian religions have, over the centuries, spawned many factions. These have ranged from the downright lunatic, cults whose sole object would appear to be the sexual gratification of those who lead them, to sects who have interpreted the Scriptures to suit their own ways of thinking. Most of these are pretty harmless and don't affect the lives of We Of Little Faith too much. Certainly not the life of this old codger: having graduated in my old age from the disciplines of organized religion to relaxed paganism, I find that I can view my fellow human beings with a pretty tolerant eye, regardless of their religious beliefs and without causing deliberate offence to any.

But there are times when even we harmless sinners can cause unintentional offence even in traditionally peaceful parts of our own country, as the following story from my youth may illustrate:

A Glasgow visitor to the Hebridean island of Tiree, arriving by boat at midday of a Sunday after a bibulous night in the city, set about finding a pub in which he could restore the tissues with a much needed hair of the dog. It soon became apparent to him that if there were any pubs on the island, the populace were keeping them well under wraps. Asking a passing church-goer where in the name of God he could find one, he was severely reproached: 'On Tiree, we believe that drinking on the Sabbath Day is a sin.' Glaswegians are rarely short of an appropriate reply, even when suffering from monumental hangovers. Our hero was no exception. He riposted: 'But the Bible says that Christ Himself drank wine on a Sunday.'

The good man from Tiree eyed the visitor coldly. 'Well,' he said, 'He may have got away with that sort of behaviour in Jerusalem, but he wouldn't have got off with it in Tiree.'

The entrenched conviction of the early missionaries who descended on the shores of the White Man's Grave that juju was an evil to be eradicated at all costs was one of their greatest mistakes. What they had failed to recognize was that the African of the coastal swamps and forests, primitive though he may have been, was basically a deeply religious person, and had been so long before the emissaries of the white man's god arrived on his doorstep to tell him what an ignorant heathen he was. It was just that he had a slightly different approach to the whole concept of religion. It was true that, unlike the white man with his solitary god, the black man had gods in charge of everything on earth, lesser gods of the forest, of the water, of the fishes, of the animals. He had minor gods of blacksmiths, of hunters, of fishermen, of the wind, of the rains, of thunder and of lightning. There were literally dozens of these junior gods, each one commanding some important facet of the forest African's life. It seemed the sensible approach: the responsibility of looking after everything on earth as well as taking care of his celestial duties would have been just too great a burden to dump on the shoulders of any single deity.

Where the two ideologies did find a meeting point was in the black man's belief that there was a god in charge of the whole shebang and that he had his seat away up in the blue beyond. He controlled everything, and, just like the white man's god, the way to keep him in good humour was for ordinary mortals to constantly tell him what a very fine fellow he was. Also, as in the case of the white man's god, the African could be assured that his god would be on his side during any dispute with his neighbour, for everyone knew what a damn bad rascal his neighbour was and that only the most malevolent of spirits would bother to support *him*. He also had the comfort of knowing that, should hostilities break out, his god of all gods would not only condone but encourage the slaughter of the opposition by fair means or foul until nothing remained of the forces of evil but blood and guts and the sequestration of their lands and properties by the victor.

So far, so good. But it was after this point that serious differences began to become evident.

The black man's belief about what would be appropriate for the propitiation of his senior god was a perfectly logical one: only the best would do. Nothing less than that. The ultimate sacrifice was required, and the ultimate sacrifice was man, woman or child. Preferably, someone else's man, woman or child. At certain times of the year, it was required that human beings be ceremonially killed to keep their god 'sweet'. It was a perfectly simple dogma and it was so easy to understand as to be perfectly acceptable by god and pagan alike.

Less easy to comprehend was the white man's approach to the propitiation of *his* god, yet it was one that he expected his black converts to accept without question or equivocation.

For a start, the white man's sole sacrifice was a turkey. Nothing more than that. Just this one bird, foolish above all other birds and respected by none, stringy as the little grey monkeys that lived in the arid savannah lands where no trees grew and much less edible. Yet, on the twenty-fifth day of December each year, this hottest of all days, when certain foolish tribes in the north worshipped their sun god, this scraggy bird had to be slaughtered and eaten. Furthermore, the reason for this penance was apparently to celebrate the birth a long, long time ago of the son of the white man's god to an already happily married carpenter's wife who, remarkably, had managed to remain a virgin throughout the conception and subsequent birth.

It was all very mysterious, but then the bush African always did like a good mystery story. After all, the dark, arcane forests around him reeked of mystery. So he had no real difficulty in coming to terms with this part of the deal. What he did find difficult to accept initially was that, in exchange for taking on board this new religion, he was being asked to forsake all his own gods, all his age-old beliefs, the tribal jujus and the colourful ceremonies of his chiefs and witchdoctors. Worst of all, it was required that any wives he may have had in his household over and above the solitary one allowed him by the white man's god should be made redundant forthwith and turfed out of the home. 'But where do I send them? What do I do with them? How will they survive without me? Without the food I give them?' was the outraged wail. 'And what will happen to their children? *Our* children?'

What, indeed? But it was to little avail. These early missionaries were as intransigent as they were adamant. 'Accept Him and His laws,' they insisted, 'or the Kingdom of Heaven will be denied you.'

It was not surprising that these early bible-thumpers – mostly, it has to be said, of the Protestant faith – made little impact upon the bush African. The Catholic missionaries, when they arrived on the scene, made an immediate impact. They were less obtuse. They not only tolerated, but made use of, the more constructive aspects of juju. They had two other great advantages over the Protestants, and these were to pay them great dividends in capturing the hearts and souls of these coastal tribes: their priests were far more approachable and much more understanding of the every-day trials and tribulations of their flock; and their vestments and music, too, had a colour and gaiety about them totally lacking within the austere formality of the Protestant Church. The bush African was ever a happy and colourful person, and he was always at his best in the company of happy and colourful people.

They certainly didn't come more colourful than the

priests I encountered during my years on the Coast. A few names spring readily to mind – Fathers Ned Donovan, Eoin McKenna, Bob Hales, Ricky Devine – but I could name many more. A few, such as Sean O'Mahoney of Nigeria and the Dutch Father Anthony of Cameroon, became so involved with their adopted lands and their peoples that their names will forever be enshrined in the history of West Africa.

They were all genuinely good people, those priests, and I have nothing but the greatest admiration and respect for them, as did every African who ever had anything to do with them. Perhaps a large part of their appeal to the ordinary African was the fact that they were tough but fair. They worked extremely hard, but they also knew how to enjoy themselves. They had a ribald sense of fun, which never failed to strike a chord with the fun-loving African. Their ways of attracting converts could sometimes be unorthodox, especially in the early days. A very old priest once told me that when he was a young man the most important item in his kit when trying to establish a mission in some remote village was not his bible but a football. 'Chuck that down in the village compound,' he explained, 'and within minutes everyone – even the old mammies – would start kicking it around. Next day hunters, farmers and fishermen from miles about would be there to join in on the fun. A few days of this activity, then out came your bible and you were home and dry!'

Their hospitality – even to those such as myself who were not of their faith – was unbeatable. Some of the best nights I have ever had in my life were in those tiny missions. The food was simple but good, drink of some kind was always available, and the entertainment outstanding. Many of the priests were good vocalists and musicians, and most of them could tell a story or two.

I have a vivid memory of dear old Father Anthony telling me how, in his younger days in Cameroon, his had been the task of building schools and clinics and churches in remote areas. These were invariably very simple affairs, the extent to which they were ever fully completed dependent entirely upon how much money was in the kitty. The churches and schools usually ended up with four walls and a roof only, the walls being of mud-block faced with cement and the roof consisting of sheets of corrugated iron. The floor was generally the last to be cemented, and would remain just a mud floor until – or if – money became available.

He remained in the area for a couple of years after building his first church, giving Mass in it every Sunday. Soon after his first Sunday he began to notice a series of curious dark patches developing on the mud floor. They were of a not unattractive mahogany hue that seemed to grow larger and larger, spreading slowly over the floor with each passing week, acquiring, with time, a rather handsome patina. Eventually, he discovered the cause: the African women in the congregation brought their babies with them, slung on their backs. Enteric ailments were rife among children in that part of Cameroon, and whenever a mother sensed that her offspring was about to evacuate its bowels she would haul it round and point its bottom at the floor. The deed completed, she would then carefully rub the liquid mess into the mud floor with the flat of her bare foot. One got used to the smell, the Father said, especially as ducks and cows often took shelter in the place at nights and they would add their own variegated contributions to the stippling. By the time he left the area, he asserted, the little church had a floor like polished dark serpentine, and people used to come from far and near to admire it.

Father Anthony was near the end of his allotted time in Africa when I knew him, and he was due to return to the land of his birth to spend his remaining years in a retirement home for elderly priests. I used to call at his little mission in Muyuka on the odd occasion and he would talk wistfully of Holland and the beauty of the fields of 'bullubs' – as he called the tulips – in his native land. Soon after my last visit, he departed. Shortly after arrival in Holland, while under-going a routine medical check, something unpleasant was discovered. He returned to his beloved Cameroon to die.

I dropped in to see him on his return. He was as cheer-ful as ever. I had brought with me a bottle of whisky and we sat in his bedroom drinking and talking about old times. As I was about to leave, he told me that he had a problem. 'What is it, Father?' I asked, wondering just what I was going to say to him if he got on to the subject of his illness. 'Well,' he said, 'we have recently been intercepting certain kinds of unwanted mail that is being sent to individuals in our school. Today we found a publication intended for one of the pupils, and it is one that is banned by our church.' He opened his locker and handed me a *Playboy* magazine.

'Please hide it under your coat as you go out, Don,' he beseeched, 'and burn it when you get home. I hate to think of the youth of this beautiful country being corrupted by this American rubbish.'

'Certainly, Father,' I assured him with a straight face. 'I shall do as you say.'

As I was about to go down the verandah steps into the African night I felt his hand on my shoulder. I turned, and

his lined old face was serious in the fitful glow of the verandah light.

'There's a very good one on page ninety-eight,' he whispered.

I was out of the country at the time of Father Anthony's
funeral, but I was told that the twelve miles of road to his
graveside on the slopes of beautiful Mount Cameroon were
lined with men, women and children as they followed his
coffin every inch of the way in pouring rain. Although it was
a year after the event, the old African lady who was telling
me about it could hardly do so for sobbing.

Sleep well, old timer. Perhaps we shall meet one day
among the Heavenly bullubs. I doubt if *Plabyboy* will bother
us there. But the crack will be good, if we can keep out of
earshot of the Head Gardener.

The Irish priests, as might have been expected, were the
greatest of raconteurs, and they could be quite irreverent
with it. They were never slow to have a good-natured prod
at their oldest rivals in the theology stakes, either. One old
Father told me the tale of a novitiate nun who, on being
asked by her Mother Superior what she had been before she
had decided to become a nun, replied calmly: 'A prostitute.'
The Mother Superior nearly had a stroke. 'What did you
say?' she cried. 'A prostitute,' repeated the young Sister. The
Mother Superior crossed herself hastily and whispered:
'Thanks be to God. I thought for one terrible moment you
said "A Protestant".'

They were perfectly capable of telling one against
themselves and their deeply entrenched beliefs, too. A
young priest entertained a St Pat's Day gathering at which I

was present with a scandalous story about a Cardinal who had died suddenly and unexpectedly in Rome. On reaching heaven, he asked for special dispensation to return to earth for one night only, as he had been on the verge of completing a most important assignment for His Holiness when he had been called so abruptly to his Maker. His request was granted. On his return to the Vatican, all his former colleagues were gathered around the sitting room, eager to hear at first hand his initial impressions of heaven. Finally, one of them broached the subject that was on everyone's mind: 'What is HE like? Is He very fierce? Does He have long, flowing white hair and a long straggly beard like in all the old paintings?'

The Cardinal took a sip at his wine. 'Well,' he replied slowly, 'for a start, She's black.'

Some of the younger priests had a decidedly frisky side to them, and it was one that invariably surfaced on those rare occasions when they were able to escape from the humdrum confines of mission life. I was present on one of those memorable occasions in the town of Okitipupa, in southern Nigeria. I had been playing football in the town earlier that day, and in the team with me had been three Irish priests. We were all in urgent need of a beer after the game and so we had called at a local bar. It was a pretty grotty little place, which, in addition to warm beer, offered the usual clutter of market paraphernalia. The Reverend Father Andy Finicane (a nom de plume, for he is now, I am told, a senior and much revered member of his church in Nigeria, and I do not think, therefore, that he would appreciate my revealing his real name) pointed to some vaguely familiar purple packets behind the wire netting covering the front of the counter. 'See what I see, Don?'

'Yes,' I said cautiously. 'What of them?'

'French letters,' he informed me with satisfaction, 'and I'm going to buy one!'

'What on earth do *you* want with one of those things?' I asked in astonishment.

'Well,' he replied with a wicked smile, 'I'm going to put it in an envelope and post it off to wee Joby.'

I knew the priest to whom he was referring: the Reverend Father Joby Kilrane (again, a nom de plume) who lived in a mission far upcountry. Joby Kilrane was one of the nicest people anyone could wish to meet; too nice, in fact, some of his colleagues used to maintain, to be a priest in Africa. He neither drank nor smoked, and he was truly one of the world's innocents.

'But why?' I asked, even more bewildered now.

'Because,' chortled this playful Father, 'Joby doesn't know his arse from his elbow. It will take him ages to figure out what the hell it is!'

The condom was purchased, put in an envelope, and duly despatched. By the following morning I had completely forgotten the incident.

A month or so later I was passing through the northern town in which Father Kilrane had his parish. I had not seen him in a long time, I recalled, so I decided to pay him a visit.

We talked for a bit, then he said accusingly, 'I don't suppose you had anything to do with sending me that awful thing in the purple packet, did you?'

It was then that I remembered my day out in Okitipupa with his colleagues. 'What awful thing?' I asked innocently. He gazed at me uncertainly for a brief moment, then he said, 'No, I guess not. I have always suspected the Reverend Father Finicane, even though he tried to blame you for it.

'Any prank that has the mark of the divvil on it is usually his doing.'

He told me the sequel. His cook, an old man whose claim to fame was that he had worked at one time for Sir John McPherson, Nigeria's Governor General, had brought the letter in from the local post office. There was, fortunately, no one else in the living room but the Father at the time. He had been puzzled initially by the contents of the envelope, assuming at first sight that it was some kind of a balloon. He decided to see if he could blow it up. It did not, he discovered, blow up easily, for the material from which it was made was unusually strong. However, he persevered, and he was making satisfactory progress when the object left his fingers as though fired from a cannon. It shot across the room in a jerky, looping flight, to smack with a soft splat against the wall by the door before collapsing on the floor in limp obscenity just as the old cook entered the room.

The old man looked at the condom lying on the floor by his feet.

He looked up with a mixture of accusation and pity and disbelief at the Reverend Father Joby Kilrane. Then he shook his grizzled head sadly.

'No be like dis,' he remarked lugubriously, 'when I work for de Gubbernor General!'

It was the afternoon of 24 December 1965. I had decided to spend Christmas with the Reverend Father Patrick Keeley. He and I had been good friends since we had arrived, almost at the same time, in West Africa, about a dozen years previously.

Irele was a small town in the swamps of southern Nigeria. It did not have a lot going for it except fish and goats and sheep and the odd small herd of little black African cattle. The very occasional unkempt clump of rubber and cocoa could be seen here and there sprouting out of the surrounding bush, planted in a rush of enthusiasm at some time in the past under the guidance of a keen young colonial agricultural officer. The moment he departed to the United Kingdom, never to return again, the rush of enthusiasm had evaporated and everything had returned to slumberous normality. Now, although the trees had attained maturity, the rubber remained untapped and the cocoa pods rotted where they fell. WAWA was an old and rather cynical colonial expression: 'West Africa Wins Again'; it was all too often appropriate.

The land around Irele, being swampland, was low-lying and flat, and consequently the road leading into the town tended to be under water for a large part of the rain season. With so much water in the area, it was alive with mosquitoes. In addition, the amount of livestock wandering around the town and its environs meant that every blade of grass and every bit of bush was infested with ticks, while in the dry season it was as hot as the bowels of hell.

It had been Paddy's task to get a mission going in Irele a couple of years back and, as I had been in the habit of dropping in to see him when time permitted, I had seen his mission in its various stages of construction. Paddy was good company; any time I felt a bit down in the dumps his sense of fun and his cold beer were an irresistible combination.

This was the height of the dry season and the sun was scorching the grass. Every single living creature had taken off into the shadows of whatever trees or patch of bush they could find. We sat in the shade of the verandah drinking, talking and joking, Paddy with the inevitable cigarette never far from his mouth.

The sun had begun to sink over the Irele creeks. The evening shadows were becoming longer and longer and the cattle and sheep had emerged to crop the grass of the little football field before us. A small flight of pure white egrets alighted gracefully and gently on the field to feed on the hordes of grasshoppers that lived on it. They moved steadily forward in phalanyx on their long skinny legs, stabbing every now and then at the ground with their sharp yellow beaks. 'Christmas birds', the local converts called them, because the virginal white of their plumage made them think of angels' wings and because the birds always arrived just before Christmas, only to vanish again in January.

Night settled upon Irele. We ate dinner and then Paddy excused himself. He had to go to his room to prepare himself for Midnight Mass, he told me. 'But you stay here,' he said, 'and we'll have another drink together when I get back.'

He emerged from his room just before midnight, clad in his vestments. 'See you soon,' he called back over his shoulder as he bustled off. I eyed the whisky bottle beside me. After a month of abstinence, its amber glow was beguiling. I pushed it away and walked down the verandah steps, following the path to the little church nearby.

The church was still incomplete, consisting only of the usual four walls and a roof, with just the empty gaps in the walls for the door and the four windows. The place was packed. I sat down on a bench at the back beside a little boy. Through the four window cavities I had a marvellous view of the glorious night sky agleam with stars, galaxy upon galaxy upon galaxy of them, with myriad tiny jewels in between, pinpricks of light around the shimmering galactic splendour of colour against the blue-black of the heavens.

Paddy was engrossed in the ceremony of the Mass and the congregation were murmuring with him. By the light of the paraffin lanterns the white of his garments was as pure as that of the plumage of the Christmas birds out on the field earlier that day.

I felt something brush against my ankle. I looked down to see some scrawny chickens pecking at invisible things on the dirt floor. A movement to my left caused me to switch my gaze to one of the windows. A goat had jumped up on the ledge to view the assembly of humans before it with yellow, satanic eyes.

The congregation had begun to recite the Lord's Prayer. The little boy beside me, his huge eyes fixed on Paddy and shining whitely in the reflected light, spoke loudly and solemnly:

> Our Fadder,
> Witchcraft in Hebben,
> Harlot be Dy name . . .

The goat on the window ledge blatted lewdly and defecated explosively, the little black pellets skittering down from the ledge to the floor beneath. It had been joined by another goat, equally satanic-looking. Both of them gazed intently at the worshippers as though they would have liked to join them but dared not.

The congregation had started to sing, hesitantly, discordantly. The rim of a huge African full moon was now just making itself visible beyond the silhouettes of the clump of tall rubber trees behind the football field. There was a pleasant harmattan chill in the night air, and I was glad I was wearing my bush jacket.

I gazed again at the goats on the window ledge and the chickens scratching among the feet of the worshippers. The singing was louder now, more confident and certainly more melodic. The congregation had begun to get their act together. The black faces around me looked even blacker in the weak light of the lanterns and their teeth shone as they sang with obvious joy about that happening long ago in a far-off land, an event whose significance these simple people could surely not possibly comprehend.

And then I thought, perhaps they understood the significance of it an awful lot better than did most of we white people from our more sophisticated backgrounds, for whom Christmas had come to be nothing but a round of meaningless social gatherings, of noisy dinners where the wearing of ridiculous paper hats and bacchic pleasures had become almost obligatory.

Perhaps, indeed, that night at Irele was not so far removed from the real thing. Simple people had rejoiced in simple ways then, too, a couple of thousand years ago on the west bank of the Jordan. And I, for one, should not be too surprised to learn that there had been chickens scratching around the floor and goats defecating on window ledges in that manger in Bethlehem on that night when Himself first opened His eyes to gaze upon this sinful world on which He was destined to make such an enormous and lasting impact.

9

A Quiet Day's Fishing

'There's nothing like a quiet day's fishing,' declared Herbert Hoover once upon a time, 'to while your troubles away.'

The president was, perhaps excusably, indulging in a spot of wishful thinking at that point. The prohibition gangs were tearing his land apart and the peaceful waters of Maine must have been on his mind rather a lot in those turbulent years.

But, as we who have suffered for our sport know only too well, there is a lot more to fishing than bucolic tranquillity. Mr Hoover had never, so far as I am aware, gone fishing in the White Man's Grave. Had he ever done so, even this dedicated angler could have been forgiven for thinking that dealing with Al Capone and his ilk was a breeze by comparison.

Anglers – as distinct from commercial fishermen – are

a very special breed. Just as true artists and musicians are born with their unique talents, so too are proper anglers born with an inexplicable, insatiable desire to fish. No one knows why this should be so, for it is not often inherited. It is seldom that a child picks up the virus from his father, for usually the father has more to do than waste his time angling for fish that would cost him far less effort and money to buy from his local fishmonger. Moreover, just try asking the average mother to dip her hand into a can full of live maggots or worms and see what her response will be. With the incurable angler the desire to fish had probably already been there by the time the midwife had slapped his bottom and wiped her hands on her apron after his birth. Neither the desire to fish nor the instinctive skills that go hand in hand with that desire can be manufactured or taught. They are bequeathed by a benevolent Providence.

But, even within this elite band of Men among Men, there are anglers and there are anglers. They vary greatly, mainly in direct relation to the quality of the fishing to be found in the land of their birth or – as in my case – the land in which they have to make their living.

The angler whose life has been spent fishing this tight little island's lakes and rivers and streams and canals is instantly recognizable. His face reveals all. Be he old or young, short and stumpy or long and lanky, the merest glance at his face will tell you all you need to know about him: that not only is he an angler, but he is an angler of civilized *British* waters and proud of it.

For his is a calm face, a tranquil face, with none of the stresses and strains associated with modern living that etch deep and fretful furrows upon the brows of lesser mortals. There is an aura of peace surrounding this man, a serenity that advertises to the unenlightened the benisons to be derived from long, drowsy summer days spent in doing nothing more arduous than casting artificial flies of impossible hues across the waters of the Itchen and the Spey, or sitting on a little stool by the edge of a canal in Essex far from the wife and the kids, hoping against hope that his dreams should not be disturbed by anything so untoward as having a fish happen along his way to suck at the dollop of gunge attached to the hook at the end of his line.

The British angler's world is a happy, carefree world, whether he be of the salmon and trout aristocracy or of the humble carp nether regions. Indeed, it could be said with some truth that the only real distinction between those two types of angler is that the former, in dress, facial appearance and physique, tends to lean towards the keen, alert, Sherlock Holmes arch-variety of our *Homo sapiens* species, with that healthy, ruddy complexion sometimes unkindly described by plebeians as a Distillery Tan, while the man who, for reasons best known to himself, chooses to pursue mudfish such as carp and bream and tench on windswept meres and canals is inclined to be sturdily rotund of shape and casual of attire, with a rubicund glow about him that can only be acquired through much close association with the marvellous hops of Old England.

These are men who have discovered the Secret of Life, and we of the Tropics who have never had the good fortune to be blessed with such inner repose can only doff the ancient topee in silent respect.

Let us compare the British angler's approach to life with the demeanour of he who has practised his sport in the African rainforests. This man has a haunted look. His is the face of a man who must remain constantly on the alert. His eyes, one notes with pity, seem to have moved from the alignment God presumably gave them at birth. Following the example of the flounder family, but in reverse direction, they seem to have migrated. He now has an eye fixed firmly on each side of his head. Not only that, but they have become chameleon-like in their mobility. In times of stress, they rotate independently of each other. This enables him to look up, down, sideways, back and front simultaneously, a tremendous advantage when one is walking along the average river bank in the heart of the Dark Continent.

The knowledge that almost certain death awaits him if an unkind quirk of fate should so decree as he follows his chosen sport has given this man a definite wariness of disposition. And who shall blame him? All of his angling life out there he is confronted by the fear that one careless step might very well arouse the ire of some nameless horror with steel-trap jaws lurking in the undergrowth right there in front of him, one casual hand upon the branch of that bush beside him results in such a charge of venom being injected into him that he has, if he is lucky, about half an hour left on this earth to make peace with his Maker.

It almost happened to me once. I had been out fishing on a river in Nigeria accompanied by a young African. He had never seen a spinning rod before and he was anxious to try mine. Amused by his enthusiasm and his impatience to have a go, I handed the rod to him. I should have known better. His first cast was delivered with a verve that would not have disgraced the cricketer Freddy Trueman in his prime. The lure was halfway across the river and travelling at something approaching the speed of light when I remembered that this was my favourite – and most expensive – spoon. My agonized cry coincided exactly with my silver darling smashing into a large thorn bush on the opposite bank with the irretrievable finality of a rogue spacecraft hitting the surface of Pluto, There it swung in glittering splendour while folds of nylon line settled gracefully among the thorns around it.

A certain amount of heated discussion ensued as to who should have the privilege of crossing the river to retrieve my lure. I was emphatic that, since he had been responsible for putting it there, he should wade across to disentangle it. I pointed out that the water was only waist deep at its deepest point, so far as could be ascertained from where we stood. He was equally emphatic that, although the water might very well only be waist deep, all manner of abominations were reputed to be lying in wait under the surface, and he was damned if he was going to risk his young life for the sake of a piece of shiny metal on the end of a fishing line. With that, he stalked off.

I entered the water, trying not to think about the subaquatic life that might now be zeroing in on parts of my body that had suddenly become very precious to me. A large, smooth boulder jutting out of the water midway across looked an attractive resting point. I had just put my hand on it when an explosive hiss chilled my blood. A huge black cobra that had been sunning itself on the rock slid smoothly into the water. It idled in the current a short distance away, head held high, watching me, its cold brown eyes like the glass eyes of a voodoo doll. Then it about turned and swam leisurely off. My heart started beating again.

Understandably, such constant association with nature at her rawest cannot help but leave its mark on a chap. The rainforest angler is full of neuroses. The sudden chirrup of a cricket in the leafy bough above his head is enough to make him skip like a gazelle, while the shriek of a parrot in his ear as he crawls, every nerve twanging like the strings of a harp, through a dank tunnel of vegetation en route to his favourite pool on the river is enough to induce a massive coronary within him before he is even halfway up the nearest palm tree.

To the obvious query: 'Why, then, does he do it?' the only answer one can give is the equally obvious hoary old cliché – 'Because it is there.' Indeed, if you have had to ask the question in the first place, then you have not been born with the blood of the angler in your veins. No true angler, be he out in the middle of Labrador or lost in the wastes of Sussex, can look at an expanse of water without wondering what great piscine treasures it might contain. From that point on it is but a short step to musing upon what would happen were one to cast a Jock Scott or a Hairy Mary out into the current and let the fly drift gently down to where the water swirls behind that overhanging branch . . .

It is an undisputed fact that the equatorial freshwater angler is the rarest and strangest of our great family of anglers. He is, also, almost always expatriate in origin, and from one particular nationality at that: British. The African of the interior has little time for the niceties of angling. He prefers dynamite, or, if he cannot immediately lay his hands on a case or two of explosives, quick-acting poison will suit him fine. Fish traps and harpoons have their place, of course, but his is the mentality of the trawler skipper and the more the merrier is his motto. The French and Lebanese, nationalities featuring prominently in the towns and cities of the Coast, are ever practical where matters relating to food and its procurement are concerned, and they also tend to favour mass destruction at minimum effort and zero risk to themselves.

Other than the indefatigable British, therefore, I have met very few for whom the thrill of the screaming reel where no white man has cast a fly or trolled a lure before to have had the slightest attraction. Most anglers I bumped into on the rivers of West Africa were as British as Izaac Walton. I can think of no other civilized nationality eccentric enough to consider risking life and limb in such boiling heat and atrocious conditions in order to catch fish that would prove, in many cases, to be quite inedible even were one so hopelessly intoxicated as to attempt to cook such disturbing looking creatures in the first place.

The tigerfish is a good example. *Hydrocyanus goliath*. All too rarely do scientific names appear to we laymen to be appropriate to their subject. But the eggheads hit the nail with this one. *Hydrocyanus goliath*. Just roll it around on your tongue for a moment or two, if you will. This is a name that simply oozes menace. You don't even have to know what it means – it just seems exactly right for this ferocious predator with the murderous teeth and the slaughterhouse mentality.

The tigerfish is a characin, a family of which the most publicized member is the piranha. Unlike the piranha, though, it is salmon-shaped, with silvery scales that flash iridescent blues and greens in the sunshine. It can grow to six or seven feet in length, but even at twelve inches it is a formidable wee chappie. Its teeth are dagger-like, and extreme care must be exercised when handling it if one wishes to retain all of one's fingers.

Death does not mellow its fell character, either. Just try eating it. Its flesh is a minefield of small, forked, needle-sharp bones, the memory of which will remain with you long after you have had them surgically removed from your gullet.

It is a marvellous sporting fish, though, and this is its sole attraction. When hooked, its acrobatics are spectacular; it often seems to stand on its tail on the water surface, shaking its head like a dog in its endeavours to dislodge the hook.

Angling on West Africa's rivers is almost always a daytime activity, so you miss the malarial mosquito. That is the good news. The bad news is that you get the tsetse fly, the horse fly, the buffalo fly, and pretty nearly every species of biting fly known to the world of entomology. It may be that you may find yourself on a stretch of river that is remarkably free from insect life. Treasure it, for they are few and far between. Mostly the flies are with you in varying quantities, and there are sections of river that seem to be the spawning ground for every fly that ever was born. When you hit such places, there is nothing for it but to beat a hasty retreat. Even British eccentricity has its limits.

Great, flat-bodied, hairy tree spiders weave their massive webs in the undergrowth along the river banks. Their webs are of an old-gold colour, yet they are almost invisible in the green gloom under the tall trees. They are very sticky, incredibly strong, and have a resilient elasticity about them. The sensation when you walk into one is quite horrible. As you fight your way out of its glutinous strands you are conscious of the fact that somewhere behind this mess wrapped around you is the arachnophobic's ultimate nightmare. He is a spider as big as a saucer, with eight huge glowing eyes atop a head so frightful in appearance that you don't even want to know about it. He bites like a dragon, and the stiff brown hairs on his body bring out a pustulent rash on whoever touches them. The very thought of him was enough to induce a pustulent rash in most of us who had ever encountered him.

I learned an important lesson early in my African career: never, ever, grasp a leaf without first ensuring that there is nothing disagreeable clinging to the underside of it. I was young and innocent then, and I did just that. My hand was instantly afire and a most unpleasant, numbing pain crept slowly up my arm. Nausea and fever soon followed, and I had a very uncomfortable few hours thereafter. My foreman, a forest-wise gentleman with the resounding name of Michael Osse Akinmulero, showed me the culprit. Hanging on to the underside of the leaf was a small, innocuous-looking bright-green caterpillar covered in fine downy hair. It was the hair, my foreman informed me, that did the trick, although the body itself was reputed to be highly toxic. It was a caterpillar much used by malevolent witchdoctors, who ground it to a paste and mixed it with other equally lethal potions when they had domestic problems requiring fairly drastic solutions.

Hornets are in abundance alongside rivers. They like being near to running water. Their little papier-mâché nests hang like brown Christmas tree baubles deep inside bushes, making them very difficult to see. The lightest touch on their bush, however, and you will experience no further difficulty in seeing the occupants. They instantly emerge in swarms, looking for trouble and disappointed if they don't find any. Depending upon the species, the potency of their sting can vary from one that is no more painful than that of the ordinary European bumblebee to one that can be life-threatening. One species called the 'yellow-jacket' by the forest people is particularly vicious. It has killed many humans, and it will even put elephants to flight.

Africa would not be Africa without its ants. Fiery red arboreal ants drop upon you from on high in great showers, and there is an even more savage little black variety that smothers any low vegetation overhanging water. Every bite from one of those means an injection of formic acid into your system. Ground-dwelling ants make their way into parts of you that only your doctor has ever seen or wishes to see. The most notorious of this clan is the driver ant. These, in fact, are relatively harmless as long as they stick to their never-ending marching columns and so long as you keep a weather eye open for them. But, although it is quite common to find them on the move along river banks, they hate water. A shower of rain will completely disorientate them, scattering them by the billion all through the surrounding bush. It is in this situation that they reach their optimum nuisance potential, for you may suddenly find yourself in a black, seething mass of them before you realize it. Their bite is exceedingly painful, and they have been known to reduce large animals to skeletons in a matter of hours.

Walking along a river bank in the equatorial rainforest is never the pleasant stroll that it invariably is in Britain. It is necessary to carry a machete with you at all times. Without it you will go nowhere. Impenetrable masses of thorn scrub line the river bank and long, trailing, thorny vines are everywhere. Stinging plants abound in some places, and tangles of liane block the way. The machete is also a comforting backup against the occasional aggressive reptile one may encounter on the way.

All animals need water, and most animals love rivers.

The river-jack, or rhinoceros viper, knows this, and so he haunts the river verges for his prey. Never more than about four feet in length and very fat in proportion, this serpent is absolutely lethal. With his incredible geometrical patterns of brown, yellow, blue, green, red and black all over his body, those who have never seen one in his native habitat could be forgiven for thinking that this would be the easiest of creatures to spot on the forest floor. They would be dead wrong, with the emphasis on the 'dead'. The river-jack is almost impossible to see until you are right on top of him, by which time it is too late.

He is very slow and deliberate in his movements, but his strike is faster than the eye can follow. The enormous quantity of venom he injects does not only kill the victim; it immediately begins to dissolve all the blood and tissue within the body. In other words, the body is being gradually liquefied while it is still alive. The damage done to a large animal, such as man, is absolutely appalling, with severe diffuse bleeding into the tissues and body cavities before death finally occurs. Nor is it ever a quick death, such as one gets as a result of a cobra bite – death can take weeks or even months to overtake the victim. The great herpetologist G. S. Cansdale, in the 1981 reprint of his booklet 'West African Snakes', wrote: 'the most effective treatment . . . after first aid and the injection of anti-venin, is the copious administration of blood transfusions or blood serum. This can only be done in hospital.' The problem with this, as Cansdale himself points out, was that the victim would invariably be several hundred miles from hospital when bitten and – certainly in my era – would never have had the luxury of anti-venin available to him in the first place. Death, therefore, was a foregone conclusion to a bite from one of these awful reptiles. The ulcers created by the venom all over the body were extremely large and deep and horrible, The end, when it eventually came, must have been a relief not only for the victim but for those treating him and having to watch his continual agonies.

Rainforests seem to bring out the worst in some of the larger animals. Perhaps it is the biting flies that make them so crotchety, or perhaps it is the depressing gloom of the high forest. In the more secret parts of the forest one may, on the very rare occasion, encounter the pygmy elephant. This fellow is not like the great big cuddly jumbos of the East African plains one sees so frequently on the television screens nowadays, usually with a variety of scantily dressed young ladies waxing lyrical over them from the security of their safari trucks. This one is a much smaller version, with much smaller tusks. He makes up for his lack of stature by his evil temper. Young television ladies – or anyone else for that matter – trying to come within half a mile of this choleric individual would do so at their peril.

Much the same could be said of the forest 'bush cow'. This is a member of the buffalo family, a notoriously unstable tribe at the best of times. During my long and occasionally energetic life I have been treed on one or two occasions by accredited members of this family, once, even, overnight.

There are two distinct species to be found in the West African forests. One is the big black brute familiar to all who know anything about the fauna of East Africa. He is a nasty enough piece of work when he puts his mind to it, but even nastier is the so-called 'bush cow'. The bush cow is about the same size as the Jersey cow, and it looks rather similar at first glance, with reddish hair and short horns. But there the similarity ends. The bush cow is as vicious as it is vindictive, and an angler carrying a rod sends it into paroxysms of fury. It will charge instantly, and woe betide anyone unable to find a climbable tree quickly, for it will use hoof and horn and its formidable teeth to rend its victim to something resembling strawberry jam, finally – to show that is not entirely devoid of humour – urinating triumphantly on the remains . . .

But it was not all bad news. Not all the creatures of Africa's river banks were of such fearsome potential. Some days were made delightful by the creatures you met. Large, sandy-coloured ground squirrels scampered along in front of you, standing up on their hind legs every now and then to stare at you in wide-eyed curiosity. They were the most charming of creatures. Each time they met another of their kind they would stop to greet each other, kiss-kiss-kiss-kiss, quickly, front paws on the other's shoulders, then scamper on their ways again, stopping every ten yards or so to look back at the object of their affections. As they ran their great bushy tails would flick rapidly up and down, up and down, flick-flick-flick-flick, with the sheer joy of living. Beautiful black-and-red weavers hung their intricate hanging-basket nests over the tumbling waters, and when you were seated by a pool in a forest glade with the rays of the setting sun casting a shimmering, tangerine pathway over the rippling waters towards you, and the flies and the buffaloes and the snakes and the spiders were leaving you alone, it could be as enjoyable there in the heart of the White Man's Grave as anywhere else on earth.

Shortly after I had retired from Africa I was sitting daydreaming by the South Calder River in Scotland. It was early spring and the larks were in the heavens. Clumps of roseate campion interspersed the carpets of wild hyacinths and the fresh green fronds of the emergent bracken. In the woodland across the chuckling waters, birch and beech were tinted with the delicate lime green of their leaves, while the sombre dark green of the rhododendrons had adopted a mantle of virginal pink.

My reverie was interrupted by a loud and mournful MOO-OO-OO behind me. My heart, liver and lights fused instantly into one large, quivering, gelatinous mass. I spun round sharply, expecting instant death in its most brutal form. In that split second I was back in the rainforests and all the malevolent ghosts of ancient Africa were crowding in upon me.

Daisy the Ayrshire cow, gazing with watery-eyed solemnity at me from a range of about ten feet, was probably momentarily puzzled by my alarm, if indeed she ever thought about anything much at all. But then hers had been a sheltered life. Not for her the finely honed reflexes so necessary to the angler of the rainforest rivers. Buffaloes have always been in short supply in the Clyde Valley, and she could probably have walked all day through its green and pleasant pastures without catching so much as a glimpse of a rhinoceros viper.

One could see the story of her life reflected in her mien: the calm gaze, the unfurrowed brow, the steady and unhurried mastication of lush Scottish grass.

Good milk comes from contented cows, and Daisy's must surely have been of the purest quality. But then, in some past existence, she had probably fished those beautiful waters flowing placidly before us.

10

The Swedish Affair

It is probable that not all the avid readers of these pages will have heard of the Swedish Affair, and it may even be possible that some of those gentle readers who have actually pitted their wits against tigerfish and barracuda around West Africa's febrile shores may not have heard of it either. But not, I trust, too many, for although it all happened rather a long time ago and the attractions of Timpoland rarely seem to feature on the lists of holiday destinations currently being touted in our glossier magazines, nevertheless this was an event that thrust that part of the White Man's Grave – albeit briefly – into the angling spotlight.

Although very small even by the standards of coastal towns in that part of the Gulf of Guinea, the Timpo of the early 1970s was a busy little town, with a surprisingly large expatriate population. Long before any colonials settled in the area its natural harbour had been a popular stopover for

Portuguese trading ships as they sought shelter from the
treacherous squalls that swept in from the Atlantic to herald
each rain season, so it was only natural that a town should
gradually evolve around the fringes of the bay. Between the
two great European wars a French shipping company built
a port of sorts at the entrance to the bay, American and
Irish missionaries set up clinics and schools on the outskirts, and the ubiquitous Lebanese built stores within the
town itself.

With the acquisition of vast timber concessions in the
interior by white entrepreneurs after the Second World War,
things hotted up dramatically in this hitherto tranquil area.
Expatriates of many nationalities arrived on the scene, most
of them based in the logging camps scattered around the
forests to the north of the town, and they were major users
of the trading stores and the port facilities.

A huge problem for modern vessels was gaining access
to the port from the sea. The bay around which the town
was situated was almost perfectly circular in shape and
around a mile wide at its widest point. It was, perhaps, more
of a lagoon than a bay, with a narrow entrance not much
more than a hundred yards wide, and only cargo vessels of
the shallowest draughts could negotiate the sand bar that
periodically silted this entrance up. Even then constant
dredging was necessary to keep the port open at all. Most of
the ships that arrived from Europe and America seeking cargoes of timber had to anchor well out to sea, with the logs
being towed out to them in raft form.

It was not a satisfactory situation, and many logs were
lost in the breakers while being towed out or while being
winched aboard ship. This was prime mahogany country
and every cubic metre of timber lost was therefore an

expensive loss, not only to the concessionaires but to the shipping company insurers and the government. With the volume of timber arriving at port from the forests escalating by the year, it was obvious that something had to be done to improve the existing harbour facilities. The timber men and the shipping people therefore pooled their resources and an internationally renowned German construction company was given the contract to build a new harbour.

In short order, large numbers of young Germans were establishing their own camp on the outskirts of the port. A very superior sort of camp it was, too. The Germans were nothing if not efficient. They constructed a small airstrip so that supplies could be ferried in from the distant capital on a daily basis, and they built their own commissary. A huge generating plant supplied their electricity, and they had their own private club complete with cinema, swimming pool, football field and tennis courts.

Sport, in fact, was of prime importance to the Germans. They were the hardest of workers and most of them were young. They had to let off steam somehow and they had none of the traditional social outlets for their surplus energy that young Germans could expect back home, especially as fraternization with the locals, if not exactly verboten in so many words, was certainly not looked upon with favour even by their peers, never mind their superiors. In this, they had a very high intolerance factor. Most expatriates I knew in those days tended to be racist to one degree or another, but one or two of the less tolerant among the Germans still seemed to me to have the cheers of the Nuremberg rallies echoing in their ears.

They all had that very German approach to sport that

brooked no thought of being second-best to anyone.
Although it was a regrettable fact that they refused point-
blank to play against teams consisting entirely of Africans
in any sport, they were ceaseless in their quest for new
sporting worlds to conquer among other expatriates. They
would arrange matches in this and that against the
combined resources of the timber people, assorted missionaries, or whoever was fit enough and daft enough to
run around a field in the baking heat of an equatorial day.
When the local expatriates got fed up with being constantly thrashed by them, white teams would be invited in
from the capital for a weekend in the bush and a beating
on the sports field. I think, on reflection, that it may not
even have been the pleasure they got from the physical
exercise that mattered most to the Germans. What really
concerned them was being able to display their superior-
ity in everything.

I must admit that, on the whole, I got on very well
with most of those I met. But then, I did not see them too
often, for I lived some distance upcountry, and the only
reason I ever had for travelling down the awful road to
town was in order to purchase necessary supplies from
the Lebanese stores. Sometimes I would bump into one or
two of the Germans, buying crates of machetes for their
workers, perhaps, or standing in little huddles at the end
of the counter drinking bottles of imported beer. There
would be times when I would spend the weekend in port
with the French shipping agent and his wife, and quite
often we would come across them sunning themselves
on the sand as we strolled along the beach on Sunday
mornings.

It was while on one of those visits that the shipping

agent, Pierre, told me that some of the Germans had been asking him about the possibilities for sea angling out here as they had been keen on the sport back home. Pierre had promised to take a couple of them out on the port launch the following afternoon. Would I care to come along?

I had no rod with me on this visit, but it was always a joy to be out on the sea in the Tropics. Particularly here. In the open seas beyond the harbour those supremely edible carnivores, the barracudas, cruised in great silver shoals. The gargantuan groupers were in abundance, too; indeed, during the rains when the tides were high they could occasionally be found within the confines of Timpo Bay itself.

The Germans were waiting for us at the wharf. They were both in their early thirties and big and burly. One was clean-shaven, while the other had a large kaiser-style moustache. They were pleasant but very formal as they introduced themselves: Herr Koch and Herr Schütz. But they were obviously the strong silent types, for thereafter they said very little and concentrated on the fishing.

It was their first experience of fishing on tropical seas and they obviously enjoyed themselves. They could only spare a couple of hours on the water before they had to return to camp, but they were broken twice in that time – each time by a heavy grouper, I rather fancied, judging by the solid, plunging runs – and the kaiser caught an eight-pound barracuda on a big brass spoon. It fought magnificently, as barracudas always do, standing on its tail on the surface of the sea, thrashing its head around in showers of gold and silver spray before falling back down into the depths to prepare for its next launch into the African sunset.

That night Pierre and his wife took me to the 'French Bar' that had opened the previous week on the other side of town. An old Corsican timber man, hoping to cash in on the influx of Europeans to the area, had purchased an abandoned Baptist mission building and converted it into a sort of diner-cum-nightclub, complete with its own little generator for lighting and the supply of refrigerated beer. He was a tolerable cook, and he had managed to come to an arrangement with the Germans regarding the ordering of periodic essentials from the city via their little Cessna plane.

The bar was packed with white people, mostly young timber men from the interior out for a night on the town. I knew many of them by sight and they were a very cosmopolitan crew: a lot of French, but also smatterings of Dutch, Swiss, Scandinavians and Italians. At the far end of the bar from where we sat a small group of them were hanging around half a dozen exotically dressed black girls, prostitutes from the capital, Pierre's wife told me, who had come to see what pickings were to be had out here in the boondocks from these new Europeans.

Kurt ambled over to greet us. He was a big, amiable young Swede whom I knew quite well, for I sometimes dropped in at his house for a beer en passant – he lived at a logging camp twenty miles to the north. After a few moments, he returned to the bar. A record player started up and the pounding beat of African hi-life music echoed round the walls. A very tall girl detached herself from the crowd and said something to the Swede. Together they moved over to the dance floor. They stood on the centre of the floor, bodies pressed together and barely moving as other couples circled around.

I studied her. Despite the thick haze of cigarette smoke and the dim lighting I could see that, facially at least, she was one of the prettiest African girls I had ever seen. She was wearing black three-quarter-length, skintight pants and an equally skintight top of a hue so deeply purple as to be almost black, too. It was an outfit that, combined with the poor visibility and the darkness of her skin, made her seem almost naked from where we sat. She was like a long, sleek, elegant black panther, I thought. She and Kurt obviously knew each other well, and I reckoned that he would not be travelling back to bush on his own this fine night if he could help it.

It was not to be until two months later, at the beginning of December, that necessity took me back to town again. I spent a leisurely afternoon in the three main stores in town, then, having completed my shopping, I made straight for the port. Pierre and his wife were at home and I dumped my gear in their spare room.

'Have you heard about the big fishing challenge?' asked the Frenchman as we sat out on the verandah with our beer. 'I have heard nothing concerning Timpo,' I replied. 'For I did not call at the logging camp on the way down. The only people I have spoken to since leaving the bush have been the Lebanese shopkeepers, who, as you are well aware, are not much interested in conversation that has nothing to do with money.'

'Indirectly,' said Pierre dryly, 'this has a lot to do with money, for there is heavy gambling involved. But it has even more to do with honour, I suspect. German honour, Swedish honour and – believe it or not – African honour.'

Intrigued, I begged him to reveal all. And thus it came

to pass that I became embroiled, albeit unwittingly, in what would for ever after be referred to as the 'Swedish Affair'. Hushed whispers would be the order of the day when referring to it, for this was a matter that was to shake this peaceful little backwater out of its slumber and create divisions of such depth and width between two sections of the expatriate community that, for all I know, they may very well exist there to this present day . . .

Like many another disagreement in history, it all started innocently enough – in this case, a minor misunderstanding fuelled by alcohol. The daughter of the proprietor of the largest Lebanese store in town had got married and her father had hired the French Bar for the night to entertain the expatriate community in celebration of the event. Even some of the Germans – not normal habitués of the bar – had come along.

The place was packed and conversation was fairly general. The atmosphere was relaxed and the Germans were mixing freely with the other guests. Kurt and Wolfgang – a small but rather sinister-looking Himmler lookalike, even down to the mousy little moustache and rimless glasses – had discovered that they had a common interest in fishing. Wolfgang spent most of his free time among the barracudas and the groupers at the port, while Kurt had been a keen salmon fisher in his native Sweden. He had brought his favourite rod out with him, he told Wolfgang, but he hadn't had much chance to use it. An invitation by Wolfgang to a day out in his boat had been instantly rejected by Kurt. 'Thank you very much, Wolfgang, but I get seasick even if my soup has too much salt in it!' shuddered that hardy ancestor of one of the greatest seafaring nations the world has ever known.

It was at this point that the idea of an angling competition was mooted. 'Why don't we organize one for Boxing Day,' said Wolfgang, 'to see who can catch the greatest weight of fish in a specified time? Sea versus river? Germany versus Sweden? And,' he added magnanimously, for the beer they were drinking was imported Bergedorf and very strong, 'my company will present a trophy and top quality German-made rods and reels to the members of the winning team.'

The format for the event was drawn up there and then: each team to consist of three anglers, the three sea fishers to fish from stances mutually agreed by the teams around Timpo Bay, and the three freshwater anglers to fish from similarly agreed stances along the Timpo River just outside town. Fishing would be by rod and line, with whichever lure, artificial fly or bait the angler chose to use. The contest would last exactly three hours – from two o'clock until five o'clock in the afternoon – and all the fish would be taken immediately after five o'clock to Pierre's house to be weighed. Both teams would be about equidistant from fishing point to the weighing point and umpires of neutral nationality would be agreed upon by the competing teams in advance to ensure fair play.

There was a marvellous ambience at this point of the proceedings, said Pierre. Old Man Bader, the Lebanese who was hosting the wedding reception, chipped in with an offer of one hundred dollars for the individual champion, while another Lebanese storekeeper promised to donate a couple of cases of champagne for the post-match celebrations. Then – for he had to recover the cost of the champagne somehow – he stated that he would open a book on the match. Anton, the owner of the French Bar, was happy to allow his premises to be used for the revelry after the match . . .

I have occasionally been accused of being a cynic, and all this sounded to me to be too cosy by half. There had to be a glitch somewhere. Things just did not operate as smoothly as this in West Africa. Pierre had gone silent. He was sipping at his beer rather distractedly and gazing out over the sough-ing breakers towards the horizon. Something, it seemed to me, was exercising his mind.

'So?' I prompted.

'So then Titi came in,' he said.

'Titi?'

'Kurt's girlfriend,' he explained.

The penny dropped. 'You mean, his *black* girlfriend?'

'Yes,' said Pierre.

I still could not see where all this was leading. I was well aware of the barely concealed racism of a number of the young Germans, but I failed to see how the love life of young bachelors living in a logging camp could be any busi-ness of theirs.

Pierre continued, 'You see, everyone was aware that there had been no coloured people among the invited guests, so it was a considerable surprise to the Germans, I suppose, when Titi suddenly appeared out of the darkness.'

'Well?'

'Well, Wolfgang obviously was unaware that she was Kurt's girlfriend. He thought she was just an uninvited harlot trying to gatecrash the party. He told her to get out. She told him to piss off. At that he lost his temper and gave her a good hefty shove. She stumbled over a chair, hitting her head on the edge of the bar on the way down and knocking herself out stone cold.'

'Good grief!'

'Yes,' said Pierre. 'There she was, flat on her back on the floor in the land of dreams. So Kurt instantly punched Wolfgang straight in the face, breaking his glasses and removing two of his teeth in the process. Then one of the other Germans kicked Kurt's feet from under him and stamped on him. But not more than twice, for after the second time one of the other Swedes smashed *him* over the head with a bar stool. It was at this point,' continued the Frenchman with droll Gallic humour, 'that things began to turn a bit nasty, the evening ending in a general free-for-all, shit and blood all over the place, and considerable alterations having been made to the decor of the French Bar.'

I gazed at the man in awe. 'By golly, you people down here do live the life!' I said at last. 'I suppose the fishing contest has been abandoned?'

'On the contrary,' replied Pierre. 'All this has merely added piquancy to it. It proceeds as before, but with all the post-match celebrations now being held in my place rather than in the French Bar. For some reason or other, Anton has had enough of fishing contests. But the whole area is buzzing with excitement over it. Bashir the bookie is offering two to one against the Swedes but I believe that loyalties are sharply divided, with the town people favouring the Germans and the bush people putting their money on the Swedes. I have even heard rumours of heavy sums being handed over the counter on behalf of St Theresa's Girls' School, but Bashir's lips are sealed. Two of his daughters are pupils there and he fears what the harvest might be were he to grass on the Mother Superior, who is a case-hardened old dragon from Sligo.'

I glanced at the calendar behind me. 'Ten days from today!' I mused. 'I wonder who they're appointing as umpires?'

'Well,' said the Frenchman, 'I have been asked to umpire for the three Germans fishing around Timpo Bay, and I have to mark out their stances the day before the contest. I think it is intended that you should be asked to do the same for the river anglers.'

'WHAT??'

'Yes. I said I was sure you would agree; you're such a public-spirited chap.' He broke off and peered out into the gathering gloom. 'Ah! Here are the very people I was expecting – the German competitors.'

He stood up as a badly bruised Wolfgang, followed by two young men who introduced themselves as Ernst and Hans, came into the room.

It was a long and rather difficult evening. They spoke perfect English and they were absolutely charming. But I was uncomfortable. I have never felt at ease among those who affect to despise the people of the country in which they happen to be making a good living. I was glad when they stood up to leave, and it was only when they assured me that the Swedes and they were unanimous in their choice of me as an umpire that I felt better about the whole sordid deal. 'You are the obvious choice, anyway,' Wolfgang said. 'These Swedish bastards won't pull any tricks with you in charge. The English are renowned for their fair play.'

'I am Scottish,' I reminded him stiffly.

'Same thing,' he replied dismissively.

I left immediately after breakfast. I had intended to spend a further night in port, but I felt it necessary now to pay a call on the Swedes. Some sixth sense was niggling away at me. Whatever was going to happen in this fishing contest, I could feel in my bones that it would not be as envisaged by the venerable gentlemen of *Field and Stream*. Nor had my foreboding lessened in any way by the time my truck turned off the road and into Kurt's camp.

I walked up the verandah steps and in through the open door. The ceiling fan was clunking away lethargically but there was no sign of life. 'Hello!' I called. 'Anyone at home?'

I was about to return the way I had come when the bedroom door opened and a figure emerged, barefoot and dripping water.

I recognized her instantly as being the girl I had seen on my one and only visit to the French Bar. She was wearing a towel around her waist and a thoroughly wet slip that she need not have bothered to put on for all that it succeeded in concealing. She stood in the doorway of the bedroom, momentarily nonplussed, then she said, 'I was having a shower when I heard someone calling and I thought it was Kurt . . .'

Then she walked over to me, her hand outstretched. Her smile was warm and genuine. 'Hi!' she said. 'I'm Titi. You must be Don. I've heard a lot about you.'

She brought me some tea from the kitchen while she went to the bedroom to dry herself off and put on a respectable dressing gown. She came back out and sat in a chair facing me. She told me about herself in a strange mixture of English and pseudo-Americanese, the latter no doubt learned from listening to American film stars in a variety of cinemas in a variety of towns along the Coast during a colourful career. She was a Bambara from distant Mali, she told me, where her father had been a fisherman, and she had been living with Kurt for the past three months. He had picked her up in a bar in Accra and had brought her over here with him. He had promised to take her back to Sweden when his current tour ended in eighteen months' time, she said proudly, and there had even been talk of marriage.

Kurt came in from the compound. He was quite without remorse about his contribution to the fracas in the French Bar. I asked her if she felt any sense of grievance about what had happened that night. Her smile faded for a moment and she said quietly, 'I'm well used to being abused. Sometimes, even, by you British.'

I turned the conversation to the forthcoming angling challenge. 'I'll be down here on Christmas morning, the day before it's due to start, to mark out your three fishing stances on the river. This will give you a chance to have a path cleared along the river bank so that I can move freely between each team member.'

A thought struck me. 'By the way,' I asked, 'how much fishing have you actually done out here?'

'Very little,' he admitted. 'My friend Claus and I have been out in the evenings a couple of times with spinning rods and caught a few small perch, but that's all.'

I eyed him contemplatively. 'You'll be out by the river in the afternoon for the contest,' I reminded him. 'Do you know what that means?'

'No.'

'It means,' I informed him, 'that you will be out at the worst possible time of the day for river fishing in Africa. It will be the height of the dry season, the river will be at its lowest depth, and it will be as hot as hell. The big fish will be lurking where you can't catch them, among roots close into

the bank or cooling off in the mud at the bottom of the
deepest pools, and they won't emerge until near dark. The
only things you are liable to encounter are shoals of tiny
reedfish that come to the surface while the big guys are
resting.'

He was gazing at me, a sort of slow horror creeping
over his features. 'Christ!' he said. Then, with a hint of panic
in his voice, 'What about the Germans? Won't they be as
badly off? I've been told by someone that there are no fish at
all worth catching in the bay at this time of the year – they
keep beyond the harbour wall . . .'

'Well,' I said, 'the good news is that the big groupers
won't be in at this time. It's far too shallow inside the harbour. The bad news is that the bay will be full of ratfish. And
they feed all day long.'

'Ratfish?'

'Yes, ratfish. Ugly brown things with great big goggly
eyes and long tails like rats. You often see them for sale by
the basketful in the local markets. The locals love 'em –
they're full of oil.'

'Are they big?' asked the Swede anxiously.

'You can occasionally get them at three or four pounds
in weight, but not often. More often you get them at just a
few ounces. But, believe me, there are millions of them
around, and they'll grab at any damned thing presented to
them.'

Kurt was looking more depressed by the second. 'What
you've got to do,' I continued, 'is keep every single thing you
catch, no matter how small. You won't catch anything but
tiddlers at that time of the day, so keep *everything*. It will all
count in the weighing. The Germans, I suspect, will only
keep the good-sized fish. They'll be too proud to bring

rubbish into the scales for everyone to see. At least, that's my theory, and you'd better hope I'm right. You can only pray that they don't catch half a dozen big ratfish or you're sunk. With the river this low you'll be lucky if you lift a couple of pounds of fish in the whole afternoon.

'One thing more,' I added. 'Bring your iceboxes with you to keep your catch from drying out until they reach the weighing point at port.'

I rose to go. Then another thought struck me. 'By the way, who are your two teammates? You mentioned your friend Claus?'

'Yes, he's one.'

'And . . .'

'And Titi.'

I thought I was hearing things. '*Titi*?'

'Yes,' he said glumly. 'I was a little bit drunk when I was submitting the team names. Besides, when I heard that all the fish would be gone from the bay at this time of the year I thought it would be easy for us. I thought that with Claus and myself being fishermen we'd be able to catch enough for three of us. And I knew how much it would annoy the Germans if we had a black girl in our team. Especially when it was Titi. If we were to win, too, the humiliation would be all the greater for them.'

He shook his head dismally and repeated, 'I must have been *very* drunk . . .'

'Can't you change it now?'

'No. The team has been officially entered with Old Man Bader, the competition secretary. We can't change it now, because the closing date for entries is past. In any case, Titi says she rather likes the idea of fooling about by the river on Boxing Day.'

I looked at Titi. 'Have you ever fished before, Titi?'

She was carefully applying varnish of a brilliant violet hue to her big toenail. She did not look up. 'Not since I was a little girl in Bambara country,' she replied disinterestedly.

The harmattan mists were heavy on the forests when I turned into the logging camp on Christmas morning. Kurt was waiting for me with half a dozen labourers and we headed for the river in the truck. An old logging road led us straight to the waterside.

Competition rules allowed for only twenty yards of river bank, each adjacent to the other, per team member, the exact location of the whole on the river to be a matter for agreement between the team captain concerned and the umpire. I knew the river well and I had never thought of it as being much of a sporting river, particularly here on its lower reaches. It was a dour river, full of the most obstinate fish God ever created. To get the best out of it one had to fish it just before or during the hours of darkness, long after the competition was due to have ended.

We marked out the first couple of twenty-yard stretches and set to work clearing a path along the bank. The river was wide and sluggish at this point. I threw a couple of large caterpillars out into the middle of one pool but nothing at all came to investigate. We moved upstream on to the last of the proposed stances with the unfortunate insects still casting rings on the water surface with their struggles.

From the aesthetic point of view at least, this last section had more going for it. Although hemmed in with fallen trees and assorted branches for much of its length, this part of the river was quite pretty. A large shelf of rock jutted out from the bank almost to the opposite bank, leaving a narrow, rocky channel for the water to pass through to the long pool below. Growing out from our side of the bank and spreading its feathery fronds out fan-shape above the rock was a pretty little oil-bean tree, affording just the right amount of dappled shade to the rock below it. I didn't need psychic powers to guess which of his team Kurt would choose to fish from this point. 'This will do nicely for Titi,' he said with satisfaction.

I called at Kurt's house on Boxing Day to pick up his team. He and Claus were ready with all their gear. I was about to ask where Titi was when she made her entrance through the rattan drape leading to the kitchen.

It was, as ever, a spectacular entrance. Not for the first time, I wondered why she bothered to wear anything at all. Her bright pink halter afforded no more than the absolute minimum of covering required by civilized society for the concealment of those parts of her for which she had been so evocatively named, and her powder-blue shorts were positively inflammatory. The calf-length boots on her long and splendid legs were of the finest scarlet morocco leather, and the whole ensemble merely served to accentuate a face and figure that would have graced the pages of any of the world's better-class fashion magazines.

'Will this do for the fishing?' she asked demurely.

'I have no idea what it will do for the fish, Titi,' was all I could think of saying, 'but I know damned well what it will do to all the young lads at the reception afterwards. And it's a good job we don't have tsetse flies in this area; they would have a field day on you.'

I started the contest off at two o'clock sharp with a blast on my whistle. As I had feared, the afternoon was a complete fiasco. Neither of the men caught anything even a cat would look at. I wandered up and down the river bank chatting to them and trying to cheer them up.

The air was hot and the surrounding bush as still as the grave. Nothing moved and no bird sang. In fact, the only interesting aspect of the whole dreary afternoon was Titi's approach to it. Kurt – poor, lovelorn fool – had rigged up a hammock for her in the lower branches of the oil-bean tree and she lay on it drinking cans of lager from her icebox. She had a red baseball cap shading her eyes and a transistor radio blaring rock music by her, obviously not caring two hoots about the fact that her boyfriend's chances of winning this tournament were trickling away faster than the water running over the stones below. As a concession to her supposed role as third member of the team, she had brought along what she was pleased to call her rod and fishing tackle. This consisted of a four-foot-long bamboo switch, wrapped around the middle of which was a great coil of thick green garden twine, to the end of which was attached a fearsome treble hook such as the Fanti fishermen at the seaside used for catching sharks. It lay below her on the rock shelf. 'Nothin' yet,' she drawled lazily when I asked her what she intended to do with this strange outfit. 'Ain't nothin' to catch at this time of the day. Only fools and white men bother to fish when the sun is hot in Africa. Ain't that what you said yourself, Mr Umpire?'

With that, she pulled the peak of her cap down over her eyes and began to rock to and fro in her hammock.

By half past four the sun was casting long shadows over the river. I warned the men that only half an hour's fishing remained. A few tiny, miserable reedfish floated around in the bottom of their icebox and that was all. Both men looked thoroughly fed up.

I wandered upriver to rouse Titi from her torpor and tell her to begin packing up ready to leave. To my astonishment she was on her feet. Perhaps even less to my astonishment, she was in a condition of greater dishabille than she had been previously. She had removed her halter and her red boots and they were neatly stacked on the hammock behind her. Her sole attire now consisted of the baseball cap and the disgracefully inadequate shorts, and I was filled with a sudden foreboding that, given the slightest encouragement, she would discard those, too.

My arrival on the scene caused her no visible embarrassment. She was standing at the edge of the rock, feet in the water, unravelling the line from her 'rod'. 'What the hell do *you* think you're doing at this late hour?' I demanded brusquely. She did not even deign to glance in my direction. 'The sun's goin' down, man,' she replied in her best American drawl, 'so ah'm goin' to ketch me a lee-tle fish.'

My rather half-hearted appeal that she should spare an old man's modesty and dress herself decently went unheeded, as I had expected. Hoping to God that Kurt would not get too bored with what was left of his fishing time and decide to pay her a visit, I sat down on the bank to watch.

The rock shelf was covered in dried pods from last season's crop of oil-beans. These were long, thin pods about eighteen inches in length, hard as iron but light as cork. She wrapped a couple of them together as a float about three feet up from the end of the line, then she tied a small, flat stone to the line between the float and the hook. From a little leather satchel she had brought with her she produced three hard, crimson oil-palm nuts and two small jars of paste, one of a yellowish hue and the other chocolate brown. With a small knife she cut a deep groove in each of the palm nuts before fixing one on to her hook.

She opened the jar of brown paste. 'Smell that!' she said. I recoiled sharply. 'Jesus Christ!' I exclaimed. 'What in hell is that stuff?' I had never smelt anything quite so foul in my life. 'I'll tell you later,' she said mysteriously. She broke a twig from the tree and, inserting it into the jar, scooped out a dollop of the contents and plastered it liberally into the groove she had cut in the flesh of the palm nut. She opened the other jar and carefully smeared a small portion of the yellow paste over the surface of the nut. 'That should do the trick!' she murmured.

She threw the baited hook and float high over the pool below her and watched as they drifted slowly with the current, allowing the line to pay out gradually from the bamboo cane. 'It shouldn't be long now before we see some action,' she said almost to herself.

She was right. The float had travelled not more than ten yards downstream when it disappeared suddenly. She waited for about five seconds, then she heaved hard on the line. There was a violent upheaval in the placid waters, two massive jerks from whatever it was on the other end, then the line went slack.

Titi began to wind the line in casually, hand over hand, coil upon coil. There was something heavy but unresisting out there on the end of the line, something so lifeless that it could have been a lump of driftwood. When it was about three yards from us it surfaced and I saw that it was a bagrid catfish of about five or six pounds in weight, floating belly-up. She hauled it up on to the rock beside her and it lay there twitching convulsively and gasping its life away. She picked up a stone, knelt down beside it, and smashed it over the head. It had all been accomplished so rapidly and with so little effort on her part that there was not a bead of perspiration on her brow.

I found my voice at last. 'All right, Titi, time to come clean! What is that gunge you put on the palm nut?'

'First of all,' she said frankly, 'I made this stuff up last night after Kurt had gone to bed. He doesn't know anything about it, and I don't want him to know. He might have thought it was cheatin'. The man's so honest he's just plain stoopid. The brown stinky stuff is from the bush civet cat. Civet cat shit,' she elaborated.

I still could not see the connection. 'Catfish,' she explained patiently, 'love palm nuts. They will eat them until their eyes bulge out of their sockets. Even more, they love anything that smells, and the worse the stink, the more they fall for it. Nothin' in the whole of Africa smells worse than the shit of the civet cat, yet to the catfish nothin', but nothin', smells sweeter. But the shit by itself is too soft to stay on the hook, which is why the palm nut is ideal for spreadin' it on. Cream on the cake. Without the smell the catfish wouldn't know the palm nut was out there in the river in the first place, for at this time of the day he's only just startin' to think about comin' out of his hideyhole under the bank. But the smell filters all through the water and draws him out fast.'

'And that yellow muck?'

'From the coca leaf,' she replied.

I stared at her. It had all become instantly, vividly clear. Coca leaf. The cocaine shrub. I knew the plant quite well, having seen it grow in the Kabba region of distant Nigeria. It was a South American species that had been introduced many years ago to Africa, and I knew it to be quite extensively used by some savannah tribes as a paralysing agent for spear tips and arrow heads. Especially, I recalled now, by her people, the Bambaras. Suddenly I was wishing I hadn't bothered to ask her.

'Catfish come to the bait for the smell and the palm nuts, and the coca knocks 'em stone cold,' she elaborated chattily. 'Stops 'em fightin' and fussin' about in the water and gettin' the line all tangled in the branches under the water and havin' you lose your fish and gettin' yourself in a lather of sweat all for nothin'. The Bambara Murderer, we used to call it when I was a kid, it was such a sure-fire killer among the really big ones.'

She giggled at the stunned expression on my face. 'I thought you didn't know anything about fishing?' I blurted out.

'I said I hadn't fished since I was a kid,' she corrected. 'I didn't say I had forgotten what my father taught me.'

'I'm not too sure how legal all this is,' I protested weakly.

She was gazing steadily at me, her eyes hooded like those of a falcon. She began to bait her hook again.

'It may not be legal in bloody Germany,' she said succinctly, 'but it's perfectly legal in Africa.'

Pierre's house was packed. Even the Germans had turned out in full force for the weighing and presentation ceremony. There was a marked silence among the ranks of the latter as Titi's three fish were carried up to the scales. Seventeen pounds and four ounces exactly. The assorted small fry caught by the other two members of the Swedish team

weighed in at a meagre twelve ounces. The total weight of
the four ratfish submitted by the German contingent was
eight pounds and five ounces. It was no contest.

Titi accepted the various trophies and monetary awards
on behalf of the Swedish team with a grace and humility
sadly lacking among the members of the losing team. In her
short but emotive speech she paid tribute to the losers. 'It
must have been tough going among all those ratfish today,'
she commiserated, 'but I know you boys did the best you
could.' She ended by saying that she was now retiring from
competitive angling. 'It's a man's sport,' she admitted mod-
estly. 'The female body just ain't built to withstand the
mental and physical strains of fishin', especially when a pore
li'l gal like me has a big fish fightin' for its life on the end of
her line. In any case, a woman's place is in her kitchen
cookin' for her man, and that's where you'll all find Titi from
now on any time you care to call.'

Somewhere at the far end of the living room a record
player started up. The gravelly tones of Louis Armstrong
mingled with the mellifluous tones of Crosby in their classic
song 'Gone Fishing'. The Germans, I noted, did not look as
though they felt like joining in the chorus.

Seated on the couch beside a very proud Kurt, Titi
crossed her glamorous legs languidly and in highly visible
fashion, successfully attracting the most vitriolic glares of
envy from the assembled wives and looks of something
quite different from the assembled males. Apart from the
few stewards hired for the occasion to serve the guests, she
was the only black person present. She looked like a million
dollars. The sparkle in her eyes was almost matched by that
of the diamonds on the engagement ring that had arrived by
special delivery on the mail plane when she had been out

on the river that afternoon upholding the honour of Sweden.

I refilled her champagne glass. She thanked me graciously, her radiant smile effectively dispelling any misgivings I might still have harboured over the dark secret we shared. She looked thoroughly pleased with life this evening.

But then, she had every right to be pleased. What with one thing and another, it had been a pretty good day for a retired hooker.

11

Catfish Football

'The practice of witchcraft in African football,' declared one Mr Obare Asiko, commissioner of Kenya's football association some years ago, 'is unsettling our efforts to clean up soccer.'

The gentleman sure spoke a mouthful, to employ an Americanism. In no part of the world was the use of witchcraft more favoured than in the West Africa of my youth. West Africa was, after all, the birthplace of juju. From the beginning of recorded history every single facet of human life there had always been marked by the sinister touch of the witchdoctor, and there was no reason why our modern world of sport should have escaped his attentions.

All Africans love football. It is the very breath of life to them. They live for it, and there are times when they even die for it. Winning is all important. Nothing else matters. Even non-competitive matches can rapidly degenerate into minor wars and to those of us who know West Africa well it comes as no surprise to be told that the occult thrives even today on the field of play.

In my time, playing matches away from home could be particularly fraught with hazard in the hot, febrile swamps of the Coast. The home team always had an enormous psychological advantage. Visiting teams were often from a totally different tribal background and, for them, fear of the powers of strange jujus was very real. One always knew where one stood with home-based jujus. A familiar juju could be counteracted by paying one's local witchdoctor sufficient largesse to invoke an even more powerful one, but a journey into the unknown was a different matter. Also, the further one travelled from one's homeland, the more inextricably one's psyche would become enmeshed within the arcane terrors surrounding one. Malevolent spirits lurked behind every tree and bush, in the waters of river and of swamp, even in the air itself, waiting to ensnare the unwary stranger.

My introduction to the importance of witchcraft in West African society came very early in my career on the Coast. Perhaps inevitably, it came through football. Shortly after my arrival in Africa I was asked to play for the otherwise all-African Okitipupa team at Ilorin in the prestigious Nigerian Challenge Cup. The two towns, similar in size and quite large by African standards, were hundreds of miles apart. They could hardly have been more different, either. Okitipupa was an ancient trading town of the southern swamps, sweltering and humid and brooding. It was, for the most part, a sprawling shanty town of rusting corrugated iron and crumbling mud huts scattered around the banks of sluggish, malarial waterways. Its inhabitants were a conglomeration of Catholic, pagano-Catholic and just plain pagan beliefs. For the greater part of the year slate-grey clouds hung thick and low over this depressing place and rain was rarely far from the doorstep even during the brief dry season.

By contrast, Ilorin was rather a neat and picturesque town on the verge of the northern savannahs, with crisp, clear air and the bluest of skies. It had always been a sort of staging post for those aristocratic cattlemen from the north, the Fulanis, a place for them to rest on their way to the coastal markets with their herds of strange, humpbacked cattle. The Fulanis were Muslim to a man, and the great mosque in the centre of the town showed the visitor just how strong was the following of Islam even among the static population. But, as always in West Africa, such devout people were still not averse to soliciting with the pagan gods when the chips were down.

The chips, obviously, were down on this day in Ilorin. As we ran on to the pitch our leading players stopped dead in their tracks, staring in horror at a bamboo cane stuck in the ground before them. A dozen or so bright-red parrot feathers were tied loosely around the top. Nothing more than that. Just a bunch of red parrot feathers tied around a stick. But it was enough, for this was very strong juju indeed.

We had a good team, and we would normally have been expected to give a fair account of ourselves. But we seemed listless, somehow, as though the long journey had taken its toll. On the other hand, the opposition played with the fervour of home teams the world over when supported by a large and partisan crowd. Furthermore, the Ilorin players had the confidence of those who knew that the gods favoured them. The parrot feathers ensured that. We left the field a dispirited and beaten team, but we were all thankful that none of us had suffered injury in what had been a robust and acrimonious encounter. African juju, I reflected, had proved after all to be just as innocuous as the many harmless pre-match superstitions practised by even professional footballers in the land of my birth.

On the way back home that evening, over the long, rutted road to Okitipupa, our truck, travelling fast, failed to negotiate a bend. We plunged over the bank and into a swamp. The driver was killed instantly. The rest of us, nursing a variety of cuts and abrasions, sat on the bank beside the body while the truck sank slowly but inexorably into the treacly ooze and the mosquitoes battened upon us throughout the long, long night.

While competitive matches were usually pretty unruly affairs, even so-called 'friendly' games were often anything but that. Strict supervision was required if over-exuberant play was not to degenerate into sheer anarchy. A good referee was of the essence: the sight of a brawny Catholic Father, whistle in hand and calling the two team captains to the centre of the field to start the game, was enough to warm the cockles of the heart. Alas, it was all too seldom that such comfort was available, especially in the more remote areas.

Once upon a time I accepted an invitation to take part in what was quaintly termed the 'Grand Cess Friendly Challenge Match' between two fishing communities along the shores of the Grain Coast. I was not too surprised to find that I was the only white person to be seen among the sea of black faces when I arrived at the venue: indeed, I suspected that I was probably the only white person within a hundred

miles of the village, were one to discount the possibility of
white sailors on board the French prawn trawler anchored
just offshore. This part of Liberia was new to me, and I was
not at all sure why I had been asked to play in this particular fixture. I was not even sure why I had accepted the
invitation in the first place, for my days of enjoying football
were virtually over. Perhaps the reason for my being invited
to play had something to do with the fact that my houseboy
had been boasting to all and sundry that I had played a certain amount of football for other African teams here and
there in other countries. Perhaps there was some juju significance to my being invited. Or – much more likely – it
may have been that my fellow team members felt that it
might be no bad thing to invite their boss, for, being a white
man and therefore presumed to be flush with money, there
should be a chance of persuading me to part with the price
of some drink to help with the anticipated post-match
celebrations.

Whatever the motive, here I was, and already I was
wishing fervently that I was somewhere else. We had travelled by pick-up over a most terrible track and, picturesque
though the village undoubtedly was with its gracefully
arcing coconut palms stirring gently in the hot sea breeze,
there was an atmosphere here that was not quite right. For
one thing, I was being stared at. I was well used to being
stared at in remote villages in Africa. It was not every day
that a white man arrived in their midst, especially to play
football. But this was different. These stares were not the
usual ones of amused – and bemused – interest, but possessed an almost tangible hostility that I had never
encountered before. And it was an antagonism that was not
solely directed at me but at the whole of our team. As I sat

on the tussocky sea grass pulling on my football stockings I was surrounded by villagers: fat old mammies wrapped in their yards of colourful trade cloth, normally the most cheerful and outgoing of all Africans but now atypically silent; adolescent 'titis' dressed, somewhat incongruously, in green school uniforms; hordes of small children dressed in nothing at all, their usual boisterous noisiness strangely stilled on this day; and what seemed like a very large lynch party of adult males of most villainous mien, all of them armed, I noted with some unease, with very sharp machetes.

A natty African in pukka black referee's kit came over to introduce himself. He was Mr Jonah, the village school-teacher, and he was not in the least silent. He had completed a two-month footballing course in England some years ago, he informed me, and he had been presented with this uni-form and a certificate of proficiency and a shiny tin whistle by an impressed English Football Association before he returned to his native Liberia. He would referee this match according to the rules of the game, he assured me, just like they did in dear old England, his second home. He knew the halfside rule and all the rules relating to konner kicks and pelanties. He also knew the Our Fadder off by heart and we would repeat it after him before the game started. He could recite two verses of 'Eskimo Nell' and he could sing 'God Save The Queen And Send Her Inglorious'. He was very fond of Johnnie Walker Black Label and no doubt I had brought a bottle with me to help him see straight during the match?

His inane prattle soothed my jangling nerves after the baleful silence of the spectators. But not for long. He began to fill me in on the background to this fixture as I laced up my boots. I soon wished he hadn't bothered. Rivalry had always been intense between the two communities, he informed me. Matches between them tended to be lively affairs. Indeed, seven years previously, when he had been a boy spectator, a very keenly contested game had ended prematurely with one player decapitated, a spectator with a severed arm, another transfixed through the groin to a palm tree with a harpoon, and half a dozen houses burned to the ground. Harrowing though all this undoubtedly was, it was but a mere harbinger of the horrors to follow. The government of the day had frowned upon the bloody inter-tribal riots that had ensued, he said, and one minor chief and two village elders had been hanged for their over-enthusiastic participation in them. But it couldn't happen now, he assured me. They had all seen the error of their ways because God now came to the village through the medium of the recently built mission down by the beach, and their hasty conversion to His Glory after the riots had been further encouraged by the presence of a heavily armed detachment of soldiers at a camp just outside the village, placed there on standby by a deplorably misanthropic government.

'These soldiers,' I interjected with sudden interest. 'Where are they now?'

'They have travelled to their homes far off on the border of Guinea,' he informed me, 'for they are northern savages and this is their week of Ramadan. There is only a radio operator on station at present.'

I stood up. I was suddenly stricken by an unaccountable malaise. Although today was no less hot and sticky than any other day along this coastline, a frisson was crawling with icy fingers up the length of my spinal cord.

Mr Jonah, sensing my unease, sought to comfort me. Today, he assured me, we had nothing to fear as we would be in the hands of a qualified and unbiased referee. Himself. Besides, he was sure that the home team would win handsomely, and that was always guaranteed to put spectators in a good mood, was it not? Now, about that Johnnie Walker . . .

I gazed around me, taking stock of my surroundings. The pitch was about a hundred yards from the beach. It was with a certain degree of melancholy that I noted the leaden expanse of water that lay between us and the sanctuary of the French trawler. Even from where I stood I could see the triangular silhouettes of the hammerhead fins as the voracious sharks cruised leisurely up and down just below the ocean surface beyond the reef. Plunging into that sea to escape a maddened throng did not bear thinking about. To the north, west and east of us lay mile upon mile of stinking, impenetrable mangrove swamp. There was no quick and easy means of escape. The only way out was by the track over which we had just passed.

I turned to Michael, my driver. He was not of this area and, in common with most West Africans of the interior, he was never at his most joyous when far from his own tribal territory. His distrust of this part of the world was absolute. He had not wanted to come here in the first place and only the payment of a substantial amount of money had persuaded him. Now, it was obvious that he bitterly regretted his mad impulse. 'Michael,' I whispered urgently, 'when it gets near to full-time in the match, start up the pick-up engine and keep it running until we are all safely on board and can get ourselves the hell out of here before any trouble starts.'

Michael's normally cheerful face was a sort of muddy greige hue. 'Massa,' he replied earnestly, 'I no go wait till later. The trouble might be soon. I go start dis h-engine *now-now*, just in case, for I fear and hate dis place pass spitting cobra!'

The game was a farce. The oft-quoted remark of the legendary Liverpool manager Bill Shankly that football was not simply a matter of life and death but much more serious than either has never really struck a responsive chord within my soul. I have always been as competitive as the next person in my desire to win, and was particularly so in those restless years of youth. But, even then, I could adjust to circumstance. Suffice to say that the home team enjoyed a victory that, by its handsome nature, satisfied the home support. The post-match celebrations were of the most jovial. We ate baked fish until it was practically coming out of our ears, and we were seen off into the night with much shaking of hands and clinking of bottles and cries of bonhomie. I never returned.

History does not record whether Adolf Hitler ever played football for his German Workers' Party when he was in his physical prime, but I would not be in the least surprised to learn that he did so. Dictators seem to have a passion for the game. Idi Amin, as well as being heavyweight boxing champion of the Ugandan army, was a soccer devotee, while in very recent times the whole of the Ivory Coast's national team was incarcerated in a concentration camp for a week of rigorous army training by their furious military ruler for a less than satisfactory performance on the field of play. Magnanimity in defeat and the purer aspects of the great game hold no place in the philosophy of the average dictator. None were ever renowned for high ethics in anything, but very few in history proved more malignant to those who crossed them than that grisly football fanatic Master Sergeant Samuel Kanyon Doe of Liberia.

Master Sergeant Doe secured his place in the pages of infamy with the coup that led him to power in the mid-1970s. He and a gang of dissident NCO's stormed the Presidential Palace in Monrovia late one night, brutally torturing and murdering then President William Tolbert in his bedroom. In the wave of bloodletting that followed, Tolbert's entire Cabinet were arrested and tied to telegraph poles on a beach outside Monrovia. There, before thousands of their own jeering countrymen – most of them people who only the day previous to the coup had been lauding them – and, with the cameras of the world's media encouraged to record the butchery at close range, they were gunned to death. Their gruesome bodies were then displayed triumphantly in the military government's 'Redemption Day Calendar' that was issued following the massacre.

I am pleased to record that I only had one encounter with the repellent Master Sergeant Doe. It was not long after these events had taken place that I happened to find myself spending the night in a Catholic mission in the centre of the country. The army presence was very much in evidence. The young priest in charge told me that he had been instructed by the army commander to deliver a 'Service of Thanksgiving' the following morning, Sunday, for the coup and its instigators. It was not a task to which the good Father looked forward with any degree of enthusiasm, but, as his sermon would be conducted at gunpoint, he felt that he did not have much choice in the matter.

A football match had been arranged for the school

sports field immediately after the service. This was to be between the soldiers and the villagers. All those not actually taking part, including the priest and myself, were rounded up and instructed to attend as spectators, because, we were informed, an 'illustrious personality' would be arriving for the game. We were not long left in doubt as to who this might be: shortly before the scheduled kick-off a flotilla of armoured cars swept up to the edge of the field and out stepped the Great Man himself, all kitted out and ready for action.

For Master Sergeant Doe was not only keen on the game but – like so many with no talent at all for it – he rather fancied himself as a player.

It would be pleasant to be able to state that the army team got their just deserts by way of a good trouncing from the villagers, but this would not be stating the facts. In fact, the Master Sergeant had a field day. God knows how many goals he scored, but he must have broken all existing records. When Doe was on the ball, the opposition simply melted away. None dared tackle him. Who could blame them? And who could blame we spectators for cheering him to the echo each time he scored? No one was anxious to play a starring role in the Head of State's next Redemption Day Calendar.

I have the letter before me as I write. It is from the Scottish Football Association, and the second paragraph reads:

> I agree with everything you say about West African football. The future looks bright for them, particularly in Nigeria and Cameroon. If those two countries ever make it to the top level, it will be due in no small part

to the pioneering enthusiasts in those remote places
you mention, who were responsible for instigating and
encouraging the development of inter-village and small
competitive leagues in those early days.

The letter is dated 14 October 1984, and it bears the signature of the late, great Jock Stein.

I was home from Africa at the time. For reasons that
need not detain us here, I had become engaged in correspondence with the Scottish team manager, who was
preparing his side for the forthcoming World Cup series. It
says much for him that, famous though he was and busy
though he undoubtedly must have been, he considered himself neither too famous nor too busy to exchange letters
with a total stranger about football at its grass roots in godforsaken places that he, Big Jock, was never likely to see in
his life.

Places did not come more godforsaken than around
the shores of the Gulf of Guinea where I took part in many
football matches during my salad days. This was where the
'Catfish Leagues' flourished. I cannot now remember the
name of the cynic who gave them this name: I do, however,
remember that he was tipsy at the time and that he was one
of those offensive expatriates who had little good to say
about Africa and the Africans. However it was not such a
bad description for, like the ubiquitous catfish, these little
leagues were to be found all over West Africa and they
seemed to thrive best in the feculent swamps of the Coast.

On any map of West Africa one can pick out names
that are evocative of the mystique of the Tropics, names that
conjure up images of fetishes and shimmering heat, of
febrile jungles and deep lagoons: names like Lagos and

Benin, Accra and Abidjan, Monrovia and Douala. But those
are cities, cities that have been around for a very long time,
with organized footballing structures and leagues being an
important part of school curricula since football was introduced by missionaries between the two world wars. But we
Catfish League afficionados knew nought of such efficiency.
Our football belonged to the hinterland and organization
had no place whatsoever in the running of any self-respect-
ing Catfish League. Indeed, the beginnings of the rapid
reversal of my cranial hair could have been dated to that
fateful day of long ago when I was so foolish as to agree to
help run the Agbaje League in Nigeria. One season was
enough for me. Thereafter I stuck to playing. The physical
dangers involved as a player were as nothing compared to
the mental erosion suffered through trying to run one of
those nightmares.

Physical hazards there were aplenty, though, both on
and off the pitch. Not the least of them was in the travelling.
Some villages could only be reached by footpath and some
only by water. I have trekked miles to reach the former,
wading rivers and swamps en route, and I have been transported in leaky dugout canoes to reach the latter. Where
villages were connected by road, I have found myself
crammed into the backs of foetid mammy waggons along
with goats, sheep, chickens, ducks, flea-bitten mongrels and
children suffering from amoebic dysentery. (On one occasion a mother sitting near the front end of the lorry with a
baby so afflicted had to make periodic dives to the tailboard
in order to hang the child's bottom over the edge while he
obeyed nature's call. This created certain problems within
the confines of the truck, in that so sudden and violent was
nature's call within the poor little mite that the mother was

never able to reach the tailboard in time, with the result that we passengers were being liberally sprayed with the pungent contents of his bowels each time she passed us. My popularity among the other passengers plunged to zero when I bribed her with a silver half-crown so that she would point her infant's posterior well away from me on such occasions.)

Catfish Football, whether as part of a league or as a member of a team in a friendly fixture, was almost always great fun. I played in teams all over the Coast, sometimes with completely expatriate teams, often in 'mixed' teams, but most often as the only white player in an otherwise black team. I never once had a racist jibe directed against me. Courtesy and hospitality came naturally to the Africans of the interior.

Players were invariably barefoot. As a concession to this, I initially opted for a basketball type of shoe with canvas uppers and a soft rubber sole, obtainable in markets all over West Africa at very little cost. It was, I was soon to discover, a quite unnecessary solicitude. These lads had feet you could have nailed horseshoes upon, so calloused were they, and they could kick like zebras. Shinguards were of the utmost importance if one were to avoid shattered bones and the horrors of an opponent's horny toenails embedded in one's flesh.

The pitches were often terrible, almost invariably just cramped little plots hacked out of the bush. In the fecund soil of Africa goalposts grew branches within a week of being stuck in the ground, and on more than one occasion I have had to help fill in deep holes created by the feet of peripatetic elephants before a game could start. Matches were generally refereed by the teacher of the local school, if there was one, or, if there was not, just about anyone daft enough to volunteer for the job. The rules of the game, as envisaged by the gentlemen of England's Football Association, were thus subject to a certain amount of poetic licence.

Heat, and the sights and sounds of Africa all around us as we played – such are my abiding memories of West African village football. There are many other memories, some less haunting, perhaps, but certainly no less vivid.

I remember the ball being kicked out of play on one occasion. I pushed my way through the scrub to retrieve it and stopped dead in my tracks. A large gaboon viper, one of Africa's most deadly snakes, lay curled up beside it. It was obviously in no hurry to part with it, either. It just lay there, amber eyes fixed upon mine, hissing horribly. It took a full twenty minutes before some brave soul despatched the reptile with a machete so that the ball could be rescued and the game could continue.

The pièce de résistance at the post-match junket that night was barbecued gaboon viper. It was quite delicious.

Although participants in those games were usually noted more for enthusiasm and rugged endeavour than for skill, there were exceptions. A few characters of natural ability stand out in my mind as I write.

Gordon Martin hailed from the Dumfries area in Scotland. He was a tough and uncompromising centre-half whose fearless tackling and positional sense made him a most difficult opponent to circumvent. His was a commanding presence in any team with which he happened to be performing. Even more important, there are plenty of people, black and white, out on the Coast right now who have cause to remember him with gratitude for the many charitable causes with which he became associated, not always in connection with football, in his long career out there as a timber company manager. Missionaries requiring a bulldozer for a week or two to clear an area of wilderness for a new hospital or school or whatever knew exactly where to go to have their wish granted at no cost at all to them or to their missions. For Gordon was that very rare breed – a big-hearted white colonial who left behind a worthwhile legacy when he retired from the Coast, a legacy of generosity that paid no heed to creed or race or colour.

Alan Colquhoun was a bank manager whose marvellous skills in football were matched only by his natural charm and such outrageously good looks as to have some otherwise happily married ladies who met him suddenly wondering how to get rid of their pesky husbands for a night or two, and for virginal nuns to twist forlornly at their beads o' nights in their convents and think wistful thoughts of what might have been. It spoke volumes for Alan's innate modesty that none of we lesser mortals ever entertained murderous pangs of jealousy about either his looks or his superb physique and athleticism. At least, not often.

Then there were the Catholic Fathers, God bless 'em. They were as enduring as bog oak, reared as most of them had been in the rainswept lands of Cork and Kerry and Mayo on diets of Guinness, carragheen, Gaelic football and hurling – than which I personally believe there to be no two tougher sports on this planet. Gaelic football and hurling being in short supply on the West African sporting prospectus, many of them took to soccer, and some became very good at it. In Nigeria, Owen McKenna was a priest whose massive bulk disguised a quite astonishing mobility, and he was one whose unfailing good humour endeared him to all.

Paddy Keeley of Galway was a Man of God who took no prisoners and he was as unstoppable as a rhinoceros when his head was down and he was thundering in towards goal, while that amiable cleric with the saintly name, the Reverend Father Ricky Devine, hard as the Rock of Ages and lighthouse-tall, was sheer hell to contain in the goalmouth when the ball was lofted high into his flight path. Ricky's specialty, though, was his rapport with children, and I, for one, would not be surprised to learn that there are African players starring in major leagues around Europe today who were set on their road to fame through the coaching they received as children from this most engaging of priests.

There were others, too, such as Tom Mulligan in Cameroon and Ned Donovan in Nigeria, under whose guidance and expertise football flourished in their adopted countries. West African football owes a debt to every single one of them.

Although African footballers have made an enormous impact in Europe within the past decade, there were very few in my time in Africa who could have been considered good enough to have made a decent living out of the game overseas. In my own memory, there were only two of the many good players I encountered who might possibly have made it. Kaka Monday, a most talented and hard-tackling full-back, was one. Employed as a mechanic by an expatriate timber company, he played football as and when he had time off work. I saw him in action a number of times, and there was never any doubt in my mind that he had enormous potential.

The other African player to make an instant impression on me was Jig-Time Charlie, perhaps the greatest character of them all.

Jig-Time Charlie was an incorrigible showman. Short
and squat and ugly as a warthog, he drank palm wine and
cane-juice (an evil-smelling, liver-dissolving hooch distilled
from sugar cane) like there was no tomorrow. Despite his
unprepossessing features, his amatory exploits were the stuff
of legend, and the female population turned out in force
whenever Jig-Time Charlie was performing his unique brand
of magic on the field.

Jig-Time Charlie was the most accomplished ball-
player I have ever seen in Africa. He could do things with
the ball while moving up the wing at full speed that I have
never seen from anyone else. He seldom tried to score; he
left such mundane things to others far less talented than
he. His forte was taking the mickey out of the opposition,
and with what glorious panache he succeeded in doing just
that.

His home was the humid swamplands, the malarial
creeks and waterways of the Coast. He was happiest there.
Not for him the cooling zephyrs and azure skies of the
northern savannahs. Jig-Time Charlie was content to be
where the wet mists swirled daily through the gloom of the
riverine forests and the acrid stench of cane-juice hung
heavy in the hot, still air. He was the only true Catfish
League player that I knew of to attract the attention of the
overseas clubs. A discerning priest arranged for him to have
a series of trials with an English Fourth Division team in the
late 1950s. It was not a happy experience. He nearly froze to
death playing on grey Midlands grounds in the middle of
winter before tiny, unenthusiastic audiences, and so homesick was he that he even missed the clouds of mosquitoes
and tsetse flies of his native swamps. When he discovered

that palm wine and cane-juice were unknown in England and that – so ill favoured was his appearance – he could only get sex if he paid for it, he packed his bag and returned post-haste to where the palm trees and the sugar cane grew and the happy-go-lucky people of the fishing villages laughed and cheered as he turned hapless defenders inside-out in his beloved Catfish League.

Jig-Time Charlie has long gone. He died of a surfeit of drink and women at the ripe old age of forty-two, and I am reliably informed that he was delighting his fans with his superb footballing skills right up to the very end.

Several years ago I heard on my radio that the Green Eagles of Nigeria had won gold at the Atlanta Olympics, beating the might of Brazil and Argentina in the process. Their success was hailed as the shock football result of recent times.

It came as no surprise to me. I had a hunch that some West African team would eventually do it, for I had seen it coming half a century ago in the swamps of the White Man's Grave. I harbour a secret, selfish pride at the thought that perhaps all of we old Catfish League footballers, black and white, may even have played a tiny – if imperceptible then – part in the Green Eagles' triumph.

Nor would Big Jock Stein have been all that surprised when the news filtered through to him on the Heavenly Grapevine. He, too, had seen it coming. Right now, he will be organizing his own team up there in the Heavenly Everglades. And remembering how the Big Man operated back here on earth, I am confident that it will be a damn good one.

But, much as I know he would wish it, he'll have a job on his hands persuading Jig-Time Charlie to become part of it. Hard drink and free-spirited ladies must be in short supply where Big Jock operates now. Jig-Time Charlie will be perfectly happy where he is. The level of central heating will meet his approval, and alcohol and accommodating women will be there in quantity.

12

Tropic Heat

What men call gallantry and the gods adultery
Is much more common where the climate's sultry
                                                Lord Byron

In the years prior to independence most of the larger
towns along the shores of the Gulf of Guinea had considerable expatriate populations. How they entertained
themselves seemed to depend to a great extent upon which,
if any, colonial power had governed the land prior to independence. Liberia, self-proclaimed 'Land of the Free', its
only outside influence having been the United States of
America, had little to offer by way of organized entertainment, if one were to discount the horrible little dives of
their capital's aptly named Gurley Street and the occasional
massacre along the seafront. By contrast, just over the border
in the Ivory Coast the bustling, modern city of Abidjan had
cinemas, large and excellent hotels and restaurants, open-air
bistros along the pavements, theatre and dance companies,
a museum, even ice skating in one of the larger hotels –

indeed, almost everything one could hope to find in Paris, including the maniacal taxi drivers.

That curious institution known as the expatriate club existed in Ghana, Nigeria and western Cameroon. All of these countries had at one time been under British rule, and even for some years after independence these old and very British societies continued to be gathering places for expatriates working abroad. The small upcountry clubs could be rather pleasant places where the traveller could drop in for a beer, a chat, a bite to eat and perhaps a game of snooker en passant, but the larger the town the larger the club and – often – the more snooty they became. In such places the club committee wielded a degree of power about on a par with that of the Politburo and – like the clubs of London's West End – membership was only granted to those whose credentials were impeccable. There was not the slightest chance of the indigenous West African being elected unless he was of a sufficiently exalted status. These clubs were British and proud of the fact, and their committees did their level best to keep them that way. They could be snooty to the nth degree. Those who could not play cribbage or chess or bridge were beyond the pale, and on official Club Nights one dressed in formal attire even at the hottest time of the year.

Racism there was aplenty, of course, but mostly it was of the suppressed variety, even if at times just barely so. Even well after independence there were those intractable hard-liners who would wince noticeably at the sight of a black face drinking at the bar, regardless of how eminent a personality the owner of it happened to be.

There was a much related story about a newly arrived young wife who had rather more liberal ideas about the

Africans than the older brigade of colonial ladies. Her husband, an old hand on the Coast, had to gently reprimand her on a number of occasions for over-familiarity with their household staff. 'Keep them at a distance, darling,' he advised, 'otherwise, before you know it they will be trying to crack jokes with you and then what will the harvest be? All discipline will be lost. Besides, what will they say down in the Club if they hear you have been chatting to the *servants*?'

He arrived home from the office unexpectedly early one afternoon. Sounds of considerable turbulence were emanating from the bedroom: the thrashing of overworked bedsprings, and a familiar feminine voice giving tongue in staccato acciaccutura. His heart in his boots, he pushed the door open. There on the bed lay his wife, naked as a jaybird. Abaft her and in a similar state of nudity was his best friend and golfing partner.

For a second or two a state of transfixion existed within the room. The pair on the bed were frozen together in that most intimate posture of all, the husband standing in the bedroom doorway like a statue. Finally, the husband found his voice. 'Oh, thank God, darling,' he gulped, 'I thought for a terrible moment you were in bed with one of the servants.'

Sexual high-jinks may not have actually originated in the Tropics, but there was no doubt in my mind that promiscuity upped a gear or two in the heat of the White Man's Grave. Especially around the coastal areas. There seemed to be something about the combination of sunshine, sea breezes and glorious star-studded skies that made feminine hearts flutter that much faster and gave men's libidos that extra charge. Perhaps, too, the cloying aphrodisiac fragrance of frangipani flowers that seemed to hang like an invisible fog over every compound, especially during the evenings of the dry season, might have had something to do with it. Whatever it was, sexual thoughts seemed to occupy a disproportionate amount of many a man's and woman's waking hours, particularly when the great orb of the moon began to peek over the edge of the watery horizon.

'A standing organ has no brains', was an old Fulani saying, and this applied not only to the white population of the Coast but to the Africans too.

I have to state that, in all honesty, I knew of only a handful of cases of obvious adultery involving British colonials of the old school in all my time in Africa. Flirtations were numerous, of course, and few were the young married couples who did not have at least one bachelor friend hovering around the fringes more in hope than in expectation. Usually, though, old-fashioned loyalty and a sense of duty to each other and to their families kept husband and wife together whatever the frustrations and temptations. Many of the white wives, indeed, were incredibly naive on matters relating to sex and sexual needs, at least at the beginning of their time on the Coast. But they learned fast.

For a short time I was involved in the running of a multinational timber company near the Liberian coast. One of my forest supervisors was a Frenchman called Philippe, a confirmed bachelor who had been on the Coast for many years. He was something of a character, never happier than when he was surrounded by African girls. He cared little as to what others thought about his peccadillos.

He initially conducted his work from our camp near to the seaside, but this involved a drive of some thirty miles to and fro each day. I suggested to him that it would be more convenient all round if he built himself a house in the bush next to his place of work. This, he eventually had completed: a very smart wooden bungalow situated in a forest clearing far from any other dwelling. He moved in immediately. A couple of days later I visited him to see how he was settling in. As we sat on the verandah having a cold beer I noted a few young girls giggling together to the rear of the house. 'Didn't take you long to get organized, Philippe!' I commented dryly. 'Where the hell did you find them at such short notice?'

'It must be telepathy, Don,' he replied earnestly. 'Last night I lay in bed thinking about women before I fell asleep, and lo and behold, when I got up this morning, there they were at my back door!'

Philippe held a house-warming party the following Sunday. All the expatriates from miles around came to see his new home, for Philippe was a very popular man. French wine by the gallon had been flown in from distant Monrovia for the event. The little house, with its varnished wooden walls, was a splendid sight. The expatriate wives, gathered out in the compound with their husbands as they sipped at their wine, were entranced. One young couple, strangers to me, stood a little aloof from the rest. I walked over to them. They introduced themselves as the Reverend and Mrs Entwhistle, American Baptist missionaries who had arrived in West Africa only the week before. 'Call me Hiram,' he said expansively as we shook hands, 'and this is my wife Alicia.'

I studied them as we chatted. 'Typical American mission people,' I thought rather disparagingly. She was a pretty little thing with dark hair, shy-looking and with large, soulful blue eyes that looked timidly about at what was obviously a wicked, wicked world to her. She was the product of Baptist mission parents from Alabama while he, a willowy and serious man with thick horn-rimmed glasses, hailed from Mississippi. They each held a glass of orange juice. They did not usually go to parties, he informed me, but his wife had been keen to see what the interior looked like and they thought this would be a good opportunity to do so and also meet some of the expatriates in an informal environment.

We walked slowly through the compound among the assembled throng. One of the guests, a slender African with greying hair, stood on his own with a glass of beer in his hand, looking mildly uncomfortable. He beamed in recognition at me and I introduced the young couple. The husband had little to say, but his wife talked quite animatedly to the black man. 'What does he do?' she asked as we moved away. 'Mr Johnson,' I informed her, 'is a schoolteacher down in town in one of the African government schools. He is also a local chief. A nice guy. I like him. He has eight wives and more girlfriends than you could shake a stick at. God alone knows how many children he has. I doubt if he knows for sure himself. A very talented teacher, I'm told, obviously in more ways than one.'

'Disgusting!' exclaimed the Reverend Hiram, profoundly shocked. His wife made no comment, but her face was a picture in scarlet.

We finally managed to get Philippe on his own. He looked the real Lord of the Manor, standing there before his new house as proud as a peacock, a glass of red wine in his hand and the inevitable cigarette in his mouth. Alicia spotted a large brass plate nailed to the side of the house with the number '69' boldly embossed on it. 'Why,' she asked, puzzled, 'have you got the number "69" on your house when it is the only house for miles around here?'

Philippe removed the cigarette from his mouth, a familiar gleam in his wicked old eyes. 'French eccentricity,' I interjected hastily, ushering the pair of them off before Philippe could begin to regale her with a graphic description of the sexual connotations of 'soixante-neuf'.

There was no such naivety about the bush African. He and she knew everything – but everything – from a very early age.

The African of the hinterland reasoned that, since sex and housework would inevitably play such a huge role in their adult lives, it was better that the children should be aware from the beginning what life was all about. Few put their faith solely on word-of-mouth teaching – most believed that only the practical approach was good enough. Girls would be taken at puberty into the heart of the forest to attend a secret 'Bush School' under the tutelage of a few selected matriarchs. There they were taught everything they had to know as potential wives, and there many of them – depending on tribal custom – had to submit to the ordeal of circumcision (usually performed by one of the old women wielding a sliver of glass or a piece of sharpened tin). The children would remain in this Bush School for a period of two years and would be taught everything that the old women knew about the proper care of house and husband, which would include the various ways of keeping him happy in bed. She would also learn all the tribal secrets to which women were allowed access, and she would be instructed in the use of the various 'bush medicines', the trees and plants from which they were derived and how to prepare them. Just as important to her well-being, she would learn how to prepare and administer the many and various types of poisons obtainable from the forest: those that were designed only to give the recipient the fright of his life by making him violently ill, and those that were designed to kill instantaneously.

When she had eventually graduated with honours from her Bush School, she would be allowed to venture out into the great big world, a fully fledged woman. It was the custom with a number of tribes that the girl would then be allowed three years of so-called 'free time', during which she could practise the skills learned at Bush School by taking as many lovers as she liked. When this 'free time' was over and she had reached the ripe old age of sixteen, she would be required to go to her previously allotted husband for life, whether she wanted to or not.

(Boys, too, had to attend a similar type of training under the village elders, with circumcision also often being obligatory.)

A curious but perhaps slightly more pleasing aspect of this custom was that any children borne by a girl during this 'free time' would be completely welcomed into her new husband's household, with no discrimination whatsoever between her offspring and any that her husband may have fathered before she joined him.

Naturally, this was one of the many African customs frowned upon by missionaries of all denominations when they first set up shop in Africa. With education and the resultant emancipation of women spreading like a savannah fire across the African continent today, it is a custom that, if not already dead and buried, is surely on its last legs. Perhaps few will mourn its passing, other than the frisky young lads whom it benefited.

The girls usually made full use of their 'free time', and their lovers would be many. It might not have been prostitution in the accepted sense of the word – and the girls themselves would have indignantly refuted the suggestion – but a young blade who took advantage of a girl's naturally friendly disposition and departed without showing his appreciation in the form of a gift of some kind, monetary or otherwise, would have been considered a bounder of the lowest order. The retribution would be dire. Word would instantly be spread around and all potential avenues would be closed against him forever and a day. Even worse – and I heard of several such cases – a trap would be set. A friend of the aggrieved would entice him into her boudoir, only to remove from his body with a cutthroat razor that part of him that he had always valued above all others as he lay asleep beside her after their moment of passion was spent.

The bush African was a highly sexual animal. In my early, more innocent years I occasionally wondered why on earth a man with a whole cluster of wives should wish to go on the rake for even more women. But it was a fact that the married ones were just as promiscuous as the single men. I remember asking an old African king, a man with dozens of women at his beck and call, why this should be so. His reply was simple and direct: 'My friend, I am also very fond of palm oil chop. But that doesn't mean I want to eat the same damn food *every* day of the week!'

Perhaps it ill behoves we of the Western World to be too critical. There is a story related about President Coolidge who, with his wife, was paying an official visit to a large farm in America's Mid-West. It was decided that the President should visit the animal section in the morning while his wife was escorted round the poultry section. In the afternoon, the roles would be reversed. Mrs Coolidge was much intrigued by a vigorous rooster who never seemed to stop performing. No sooner had he stopped servicing one hen than he hopped on to the next one. 'How often does he manage it in the course of the day?' she asked her guide. 'God knows,' said the guide. 'Probably dozens of times.' Mrs Coolidge said, 'When the President visits this afternoon, tell him I asked you to tell him that.'

In the afternoon the guide dutifully pointed out the still active rooster to the President and told him what his wife had said. Coolidge removed the cigar from his mouth and asked, 'Does he always do it with the same hen?' The guide replied, 'Lord no, sir. He uses a different hen each time.'

'Tell *that* to Mrs Coolidge!' retorted the President triumphantly.

Customs varied tremendously even from tribe to tribe. With some, very wealthy chiefs would farm out one of their wives to a tribal member falling upon hard times to help him get over his depression . . . Women belonging to the Snake Cult – a rather sinister society operating in the coastal areas of Sierra Leone, Liberia and the Ivory Coast – would drop their skirts and expose themselves when they met a man they lusted for in the depths of the forest . . . After the death of a wife, an Ashanti chief was not permitted to have sex with any of his other wives for at least a month after her death . . . The Sobos of Nigeria circumcised their women, while their neighbours the Jekris did not . . . And so on. One wondered what had started off these customs in the first place and why there should be such a wide variety of them. The common denominator was the sexual factor. Men may have held the bulk of the cards but in the end the woman had to be the winner, despite man's macho posturing. She, after all, was the one who held the ace of hearts.

*

I was sitting in the forecourt of the Bristol Hotel in Lagos, watching the world go by. A young white man wandered over, a bottle of beer and a glass in hand. 'Dr Livingstone, I presume?' he remarked. I gazed up at him, momentarily perplexed. Then I remembered. 'Mr James Wilson, isn't it?' I stood up and shook hands. I had met him briefly a year previously at Philippe's party. He had been employed as manager of a trading company in the seaside town not far from where I had lived. He sat down at my table and we talked about this and that. Then he said, 'Remember Philippe's house-warming party?'

'I am unlikely to forget it,' I replied.

'And the two young American missionaries?'

'Yes, of course.'

'Heard anything about them since you left?'

'Nothing at all.'

'Well,' he said, 'let me buy you another beer, for you're going to need it.'

He returned from the bar with a bottle of Heineken and settled down to tell me his story. It was not a long one, but it was with a sense almost of déjà vu that I heard him out:

A month after I had left the country, the Reverend Hiram had departed on a week-long duty tour of the little village schools scattered around his area of jurisdiction. His wife, pleading tiredness, had remained at home. The Reverend Hiram, becoming increasingly concerned about her welfare, as any newly married husband might have been, decided to cut his tour short and return home the following day. He arrived at his mission house that night only to discover that his worries were all for nothing. His wife was in the peak of physical condition and she was proving the fact with an enthusiasm and vigour that he would never have suspected of her. In the marital bed and helping with her aerobics session was Mr Johnson, he of the eight wives and the many girlfriends and the inimitable sexual expertise. One thing had led to another, of course, with marital relations in the mission house becoming tense. The Reverend Hiram was recalled urgently to the United States. Mrs Hiram elected to remain behind, becoming, with almost indecent haste, the ninth Mrs Johnson. She could often be seen about town dressed in native dress, usually in the company of one or two of her new husband's other wives. She had her own stall in the local market, from which she sold the usual market bagatelle: tobacco, matches, candles, tins of pilchards, jars of kerosene, bottles of illicit gin, packets of condoms . . .

She was now spectacularly pregnant and – according to what she told the few whites who bothered to speak to her any more – she had never been happier.

There ensued a longish silence after the narrative ended. Then James Wilson said, 'You never can tell, can you?'

A waiter in spotless white uniform came over and refilled our glasses. I raised mine to my mouth thoughtfully, remembering the blushing bride with the innocent doe-like eyes from the Bible Belt of Alabama.

'No,' I said. 'You never can tell. Especially in Africa.'

13

The Heaviest Stone

A nickname is the heaviest stone that the gods can throw at a man.

William Hazlitt

It was evening, and the brief African twilight had settled upon the forest. My transport had broken down completely on the main Benin to Ore road in southern Nigeria, and I was still very far from home.

A mammy-waggon, belching noxious fumes from its exhaust, pulled up behind me. The driver, a hefty looking Ibo, called down: 'Want a lift, massa?'

I gazed up at him. His chubby face was stained a reddish-brown from the dust of the dry season road. His lorry was packed to capacity, I noted. The logo on the headboard above the windscreen stated in heavy yellow lettering: 'Man Is No Pelican'. Now, what the hell did *that* mean? I wondered sourly. Of all the daft signs – and in my time out here I had seen plenty of them – this one, I reflected, had to be in a class of its own.

I was in a bad mood. I had been waiting by this road-side for the best part of three hours and I had become resigned to a night of providing blood for the voracious mosquitoes of Benin's infamous black bush when this chap had happened along. Now, though, I was in a quandary. I could accept his offer and get back home to the comfort of my own bed sometime during the night, leaving all remov-able parts of my Land Rover at the mercy of the Mid-West thieves, or I could be brave and spend the night with it on this dangerous stretch of road, notorious for the heavily armed bandits who patrolled it during the hours of darkness looking for easy pickings.

The driver called down anxiously, 'Better come with me, massa. This place no good at all.' He climbed down from his cab, stood to attention and saluted impressively. 'My name is Jear-Box Commander,' he informed me.

I refused his generous offer to make room for me at the front by turfing out the elderly farmer who had been sitting beside him. Instead I climbed over the tailboard and into the back. Men, women and children were packed like sardines inside. On the floor a variety of fowls lay trussed in baskets and an evil-smelling goat stood tethered to a rail, bleating miserably. I squeezed down on the side bench between two vast and jovial old market women and the lorry started on its way.

The mammy-waggon is the Coast's answer to civilization's long-distance road coaches. With those words, however, the similarity ends. Whoever invented the mammy-waggon must have been suffering from some terrible ailment that had impaired both his discernment and whatever sense of humour he may have previously possessed. This had to be a man with a grudge against life, and a grudge against African life, at that.

In shape, the mammy-waggon has none of the streamlined beauty we have come to associate with our modern-day Stagecoach and Greyhound coaches. The gentlemen who designed those two elegant vehicles would have simply swooned, my dears, had they ever set eyes on the mammy-waggon. This truck has to be one of the ugliest pieces of engineering ever constructed. In its most basic form it consists of a lorry chassis on which is mounted a rickety framework of metal piping and old planks, to which, occasionally, one might find lashed an ancient tarpaulin to protect passengers and livestock from the worst of the dust and the mud and the rain. The battering suffered by the vehicle through travelling at high speed over corrugated, rutted roads ensures that, in short order, the springs are non-existent, the clutch leaps out of its socket with every jolt, and the steering wheel has been taken over by evil spirits. Brakes only work when they are least expected to do so, and they rarely operate when the lorry is hurtling down a steep incline towards a chasm spanned by a bridge so narrow that it is able to take just the width of the vehicle and not a single inch more than that. At this point, Murphy's Law ensures that hurtling at an equally demented speed downhill towards the same bridge from the other side is another heavily laden mammy-waggon whose brakes are equally ineffective.

'My brake done disappoint me,' is the most frequent excuse heard from drivers when the inevitable horrific crash occurs.

For the driver himself invariably escapes unscathed, no matter how numerous the dreadful fatalities among his passengers. The reason for this is that his cab is equipped with a little wooden side door, either swinging freely in the wind as he drives along, or tied back in such a way that when he sees his vehicle speeding totally out of control towards certain annihilation he can bale out of it into the bush and leave his passengers to meet their gods in whichever way they choose. A combination of local bottled beer and cigarettes liberally spiked with hashish give the average mammy-waggon driver an approach to death that can best be described as carefree. Especially when it is only the death of others that is involved.

The worst road accidents of which I have ever had personal knowledge have been as a result of fast-moving mammy-waggons whose brakes 'done disappoint' them at the critical moment. Burned-out skeletons of trucks littered the roadsides, and few of the major river bridges were without at least a couple of wrecks mouldering away in the sun and the rain as silent memorials to those who had lost their lives on that spot. I have a sharp memory of a particularly appalling accident at a long bridge on the Ijebu Ode road in Nigeria, in which two mammy-waggons had met head on as each sped for the bridge hoping to get over it before the other. Both lost the race. It was pitch dark and, accompanied by a young Irish priest, I had arrived on the scene seconds after the crash. Bodies, and parts of bodies, were scattered everywhere. God knows how many died that night. Striking matches whenever we stumbled over anything we presumed to be human, the priest delivered last rites wherever necessary and comforting words to the many injured wherever he could. The two drivers, it later transpired, had launched themselves from their cabs just before the collision. With the expertise of trained parachutists, they had hit the ground and kept running, fearing a lynching from any passengers who might still have been left alive to tell the tale.

The mammy-waggon logos, proudly emblazoned on their headboards, were always a source of much amusement to newcomers, so abstruse were they. It may have been that the driver *thought* he knew what the inscription meant, but it was not often that anyone else did so. On the rare occasion a phrase could be figured out if one had a knowledge of pidgin English – 'Putta-Putta Negotiator' was one such example, 'putta-putta' being pidgin for mud – but others such as 'Hell No Takers' and 'Impossible Journey Too Confuse' seemed to me to defy explanation. A headboard I once saw on charred wreck near to Ibadan – in which twenty-two passengers had died – declaimed: 'Jesus Christ Bush Piano'.

The African of the interior loved florid inscriptions, whether they meant anything much or not. He would pluck a phrase, or more often a part thereof, from somewhere or other and apply it to suit his own fancy. He was particularly drawn to nicknames, but in this case the nickname would generally be appropriate to the looks or personality of the individual concerned and it would often remain with him for life, to the extent that by the time he had become an old man his proper name would have been lost in the mists of time to everyone, including himself.

I knew many such cases over the years, and while the only thing I remember now about a lot of them is the peculiarity of their nicknames, others were not so easily forgotten. For a short time I had in my employ a young man of singularly low intellect who had been endowed by a discerning girlfriend with the splendid nickname of 'Copper Balls'. He was inordinately proud of his nom de plume. The reason for it was that, while the rest of his body was a uniform jet-black colour, a mischievous Mother Nature had contrived to paint his testicles a striking light-ochre hue, a fact that he quite willingly demonstrated to my disbelieving gaze when instructed to do so by his foreman. He had not one other single attribute worth mentioning except this freak of pigmentation but, although popular rumour had it that he was only a moderate performer in bed, girls practically queued up to be of service to him, so convinced were they that intimate contact with this most intimate part of him would ensure highly desirable light-skinned progeny for them.

Two-At-One-Time was a hunter. During my early days in Africa he occasionally obtained meat for me and we eventually became firm friends. He had acquired his strange nickname, he told me, through an incident in which he had been involved when he was a very young man.

The usual firearm among hunters then – and indeed it was a weapon still in use when I first went out to the Coast – was the bundook, a flintlock gun with a very long barrel. When fired, the explosion was like the clap of doom and a dense, acrid cloud of smoke would obscure everything around for the next thirty seconds. When after big game, instead of loading with the normal shot used for antelopes and the like, it was common practice to load the weapon with a specially made spear. The spear had a long wooden shaft roughly equivalent to the length and bore of the barrel of the gun. The shaft was inserted into the barrel until only the sharp metal head of the spear protruded. The theory was that when the gun was fired the spear would be ejected at something equivalent to the speed of light, transfixing its unfortunate target. It is true that it sometimes worked, but nothing could have persuaded me to try it out, for this appalling weapon almost certainly killed nearly as many hunters through barrels bursting and decapitating the owners as ever it did of creatures at which it happened to be pointed.

In the incident involving Two-At-One-Time, he was aiming at a young bull elephant, only partially visible in thick scrub. When the smoke had cleared after the shot and he cautiously made his way to where he had last seen the creature standing, it was to find not one but two elephants lying stone dead side by side. It transpired that, unseen by him, a young cow had been standing on the other side of the bull. His spear had passed clean through the bull and pierced the heart of the cow too.

This was the story he related to me, anyway, and it sounded so impossible that it deserved to be true. It certainly earned Two-At-One-Time a reputation that would ensure him plenty of free liquor and more than his fair share of admiring ladies over the years.

His companion was a small and silent Nupe man of middle years called Wo-Wo-Foot, on account of a leg rendered to a hash many years previously on the Niger River by an overwrought hippopotamus. Despite his deformity, Wo-Wo-Foot was probably a better hunter than Two-At-One-Time. He was a bit of an ascetic, neither drinking nor smoking, and his patience when on the trail of his quarry was legendary. He and Two-At-One-Time were inseparable, and I believe that the rather excitable Two-At-One-Time needed the hunting skills and calming influence of Wo-Wo-Foot more than his partner needed him.

White men may have been the colonial masters, but they were not free from being victims of the name-game, either. I am sure that all of us were given a nickname by our employees, but one rarely got to hear one's own, or, for that matter, that of any of our colleagues. It remained the black man's secret, to be chortled over when the palm wine flowed. When one did become privy to a nickname, though, it would be found to be highly appropriate, fixing on some particular aspect of – or, more often, some grievous flaw in – their boss's character.

I knew the Chameleon only slightly. He had been a flying officer with the Royal Air Force in the 1930s and he looked and sounded the part, down to the handlebar moustache and the whack-o goofiness of his speech. Despite his bluster, he was quite popular with his workers. He had acquired his nickname from the fact that nature had bequeathed him with a number of that remarkable lizard's characteristics. Rather short and stubby and round of shoulder, his colour could change quite dramatically according to whether he was happy or angry or sober or flushed with drink. But it was his eyes that clinched it, for they seemed to operate independently of each other. The reason was that, unbeknown to his workers, he had lost one in a flying accident in his youth, and it had been replaced by a glass eye.

There were many stories about the Chameleon. The most commonly related one – and it was probably apocryphal, though he never bothered to confirm or deny it – came from his early days in Africa, when he had been put in charge of a small gang of labourers clearing scrub behind the expatriate club. By eleven o'clock each morning, when the sun was climbing to its zenith and the Chameleon's thirst was reaching its zenith too, he would head for the bar for a quick pint, leaving his headman in charge. On his return half an hour later, headman and workers, obeying their natural instincts, would be lying sound asleep in the shade.

For a time, it was stalemate. Bluster and threats were to no avail, while the Chameleon was determined not to give up his morning tipple for a minor inconvenience like supervision of idle workers. Then he had a brainwave. He decided to make use of the bush African's inherent dread of the occult. He gathered his workers around an old tree stump in the middle of the clearing, popped out his glass eye, and laid it on the stump. When the shocked outcries had abated and order had been restored, he said, 'This is my juju. While I am away, my eye will be watching you to make sure you are all working.'

It worked a charm, to employ a disgraceful pun. Each day on his return he would find his men slaving away as they had never slaved before, casting fearful glances every now and then at the demon eye glinting in the sun on the stump. It was a situation that continued in this satisfactory way for several days, until one morning he returned to find his workers sound asleep as before. On top of the tree stump in the centre of the clearing and covering the glass eye was his foreman's hat.

Bush Cow was equally well named. Just like that highly irascible and unpredictable member of the buffalo family, he was a sulphurous tyrant. Like the bush cow, too, he was rather squat and unprepossessing, with bloodshot eyes and grizzled red hair. He terrorized everyone, black and white alike.

Bush Cow was in a position of considerable authority, and his wife – nicknamed Mama Bush Cow by their household staff – was a social snob. She ruled the roost over the large expatriate community in which they lived. They were lavish entertainers, but they only ever invited the best to their house. No junior managers and scruff like that; only the high and the mighty ever received dinner invitations to the Bush Cow house.

These were the years before the fever of independence swept through Africa. A new Resident had been appointed to the area, and in any British colony the Resident was God. This was Mama Bush Cow's chance to impress. She decided to prepare a lavish dinner in the Great Man's honour.

On the morning of the event, Bush Cow was having a round of golf at the expatriate club when he spotted a market woman gathering mushrooms in the damp patches of bush around the edge of the course. They looked exactly like the English variety, and having had it confirmed by his caddy how supremely edible they were, he purchased a bagful from the woman for the big dinner that evening.

His wife, delighted to be presented with the opportunity of displaying a bit of one-upmanship over the rest of the community – for imported mushrooms were unknown in the West Africa of those days – was nevertheless prudent enough to put their edibility to the supreme test. She had some of them cooked and fed to her steward's dog a few hours before dinner was due. The animal looked the most satisfied creature in all of Africa as he scoffed the lot, and a careful watch over his condition over the next hour revealed no cause for alarm.

The meal that evening was declared an unqualified success, the mushrooms receiving particularly handsome tributes. As they settled down in their armchairs afterwards, the steward appeared with the coffee and drinks tray. Few noticed that he looked a trifle preoccupied. He served the company and then, as he was about to go back to his kitchen, he said in a matter-of-fact tone, 'Madame, my dog done die.'

It would be fair to say that a pregnant silence followed this simple statement. All minds were instantly filled with the same dreadful thought. The steward continued, 'In the kitchen compound . . .' and there was a concerted stampede for the back door. The dog was indeed a very dead dog. He lay on the grass, illuminated by the light from the open kitchen door, stiff as a board and with his tongue protruding through his bared teeth in what had obviously been his final terrible rictus.

Bush Cow, despite his many faults, had always been a man of action. He moved fast now. 'To hospital!' he ordered. 'All of us! Now!' He led the small armada of cars at speed down the road to the local hospital where he, his wife and their guests spent by far the worst night of their lives having the contents of their stomachs pumped out by that most primitive of all medical appliances.

In the morning, shaken and thoroughly drained by their ordeal, they all gathered at Bush Cow's house for a good stiff brandy before proceeding on their separate ways. Mama Bush Cow began to query her steward further about the events of the previous night, 'When did you actually find out that your dog was dead?'

'Madame, I tried to tell you before you all left in a hurry,' replied that worthy aggrievedly, 'but you never give me chance. My small boy saw the dog being hit by a taxi on the road outside, and it was dead by the time he dragged it into the kitchen compound . . .'

Once upon a time I found myself responsible for bestowing a nickname that was to remain with the unfortunate recipient for life. For permission to reprint the following, I am grateful to the *Waterlog* magazine, under whose covers the story first appeared:

His name, he informed me enigmatically, was Abraham, after the Cat'olic god. He was to be my boatman for a survey I was about to conduct on the Anambra River, a tributary of the Niger.

By tropical standards, the Anambra was not a long river. Nor was it very wide, except at the point where it approached its confluence with the Niger at the ancient market town of Onitsha to the south. But it was treacherous and fast-flowing, and hemmed in by forest for much of its length.

My survey would begin on the upper reaches of the river, home of the turbulent Tiv tribe. Abraham, I soon discovered, was a good waterman. His one serious defect was his addiction to alcohol. Palm wine and can-can (a local hooch of horrific smell and potency) were the stuff of life to him. It was not that he was ever drunk enough while in charge of the canoe to make me concerned for my own safety; it was just that he seemed in constant need of topping up. Were it not for the drink, he informed me candidly on one occasion, nothing could have persuaded him to voyage such dangerous waters in a dugout canoe for such lousy pay in the first place.

A canoe is no place to find oneself accompanied by a man reeking of can-can. The effluvium would have felled a distillery goat. Soon I had given him a nickname, one which he liked so much that he instantly adopted it. Abraham-After-The-Cat'olic-God was cast for ever into the wilderness. His new name, he told the world proudly, was Pisspot.

Pisspot's was the happiest of dispositions. He was always laughing and joking, and never did he allow the passing of a day without regaling me with the latest hit from the Tiv Top Twenty. Although he obviously considered himself to be no mean singer, his was not a style that would have won universal acclaim. The mellow sonics associated with such minstrels as Crosby and Como were lost on him. Indeed, all airs sounded the same when given the Pisspot treatment – an eerie lupine yowl that set the teeth on edge and had parrots and monkeys fleeing in silent fright from the trees bordering the river as we passed by.

Pisspot's only claim to fame was his skill as a fisherman, but not, let it be understood, one of the Izaak Walton school. His methods, effective though they undoubtedly were, would have raised an eyebrow or two among angling purists. He knew, for example, that a few of the toxic fruit of the mammee-apple tree deposited in the shallows where the big catfish basked would render senseless every fish in the vicinity within seconds, while a business relationship with a wandering tin prospector had introduced him to the potential of explosives, thus heralding an era that – though mercifully brief – would live in the memory of the river people long after they had buried their dead.

It was for his knowledge of the river that I had hired him for my work, but I made use of his knowledge for my off-duty pleasures, too. The river was full of Nile perch, but catching them by sporting methods was not so easy unless one knew exactly where to go. Pisspot knew, and sometimes I would go fishing for them in those deep, secret places among the stilt-rooted uapaca trees where little side-streams merged silently with the river. Here lurked the perch in the cool of the evening, waiting among the roots for whatever morsels the water might carry within their reach.

Angling, though, bored Pisspot. Fishing for sport was

just not his scene. He showed no interest in it, and he would moor the canoe and lie patiently in the shade of a tree until I was ready to be transported to the next spot on the river, sucking contentedly at his bottle and dreaming Pisspot dreams . . .

Never trust a drunkard, is an old saying. When I got my come-uppance, its genesis was simplicity itself. I was moving supplies from my base camp to a temporary camp well downriver. Although our canoe was heavily laden, we were making good progress: an unseasonable storm had swollen the river and Pisspot had little to do but steer as we raced with the current.

Pisspot was in top form. We were going to be away from base camp for some time, and he had taken the precaution of stocking up with can-can – some two dozen bottles of the stuff were piled up around his feet. Finishing one bottle, he reached for another and inadvertently dropped his paddle. Snatching frantically at it, he succeeded only in knocking it overboard. The heavy ironwood paddle sank like a stone.

Needless to say, we had no spare paddle. Within seconds, we were rotating helplessly and with gathering speed in the flood. As I could not swim a stroke and Pisspot, who could but looked at this moment in no fit state to do so, this, I felt, was a situation that demanded serious and immediate practical thought. My companion, however, was giggling foolishly to himself, apparently unperturbed about the peril in which he had placed us. His was a nonchalance I felt quite unable to share, so this seemed as good a time as any to sever our relationship.

When confronted by crises in Africa, my instinct has always been to look for a tree. It is a stratagem that has served me well on a number of occasions. Ensconced within the crown of a tree and with nothing to distract one, generally, except the ants and the mosquitoes and the odd itinerant serpent, one has the opportunity to work out one's destiny in a cool and measured way, let the forces of nature do their worst around one.

There was no shortage of trees here. Their branches trailed out over the water wherever I looked. We passed under one and I grabbed at it. I was scooped neatly out of the canoe and into the river. My last view of Pisspot before I became engrossed in my own affairs was of him sitting on a tarpaulin in the canoe as it swirled at speed round a bend in the river. He was lifting a bottle to his lips.

Dahoma branches are long and supple. They do not break easily. In this, I was fortunate, for, though no more than two inches thick at the point at which I grasped it, this branch held my weight. But branches of this diameter are not easily climbed, unless one happens to be one of the smaller anthropoids. All I could do, therefore, was hang on and hope for the best. From the shoulders downward I was now immersed in the rushing waters. Although large crocodiles were unknown this far from the Niger, I had no way of knowing what other carnivores might be lurking below the surface, and it was therefore with considerable relief that I found myself being pulled ever more surely towards the side of the river as the branch bent under my weight. I caught hold of a projecting tree root and moments later I was standing on the bank.

The tree that had been my saviour was huge. Deep lacerations in the bark indicated the very recent presence of a male leopard. A big sod, too, I noted morosely: the claw marks were about nine feet up the trunk. Just upstream from where I stood I could see the tracks of buffalo and hippo on a wide game trail leading to the river.

This was a forest that would have brought joy to the hearts of Durrell and Attenborough. It brought no joy to mine. I had about twenty miles of thick bush and swamp to plough through before I got back to base camp, and darkness would be upon me long before that. It looked as though the Anambra monkeys were going to have company when they settled down to roost among the branches tonight.

The canoe, I guessed, would be nearing the rapids by now. I thought bitterly about my precious gear, lost, no doubt, forever because of Pisspot and his wretched drink. Mind you, I reflected philosophically, on the plus side was the fact that Pisspot was in the canoe and I was here.

Suddenly I began to feel better. Much better. I set off up the river bank, humming a little tune. It was not one from the Tiv Top Twenty, either.

Darkness had fallen. The mammy-waggon rumbled on its way over the laterite road, heading due west to the village of Ore and, far beyond it, the city of Lagos. There were few hills of any consequence on this road for we were travelling through lowland rainforest and so there was little necessity for gear changing. All that our driver had to do for most of the journey, therefore, was what the majority of his ilk most enjoyed doing, which was keeping his foot hard down on the accelerator and praying to his gods that his brakes would not 'disappoint' him.

In the back I had begun to doze off, lulled by the hypnotic sound of the engine. I was jolted awake by an elbow in my ribs from one of the old mammies sitting beside me.

'Old man up there is trying to ask you something,' she informed me.

I peered through the darkness, trying to make out the face. A shape came over to me, crouched double in the cramped confines of the truck, his left hand maintaining a tight grip on the metal framework above him. He held out his right hand to me. 'Wel-i-come, massa,' he greeted me. 'Wel-i-come. My name is Graffish Boy.'

Graffish Boy. Grass-country Boy. My eyes were becoming accustomed to the dark and I could now vaguely make out his face: old and wrinkled, with the thin, spare features of the Igbirra tribe, those contentious grassland people who lived among the majestic inselbergs of the plains of Okene far to the north-east of our road.

I shook his proffered hand, and he asked me if I had a torch he could borrow. I fished one out of my bag and he returned to his corner beside the goat. The torch illuminated two large calabashes, leaves plugged into their spouts and the frothy white of palm wine oozing from them. He produced two battered old tin mugs and filled one of them. He drank carefully and ostentatiously in the traditional West African gesture to show everyone that the imminent offering was safe to drink. Then he refilled the mug and passed it round to me. The second mug he also filled and handed it to the passenger sitting next to him. 'Let we all drink and sing this night,' he said. 'We got far to travel and we may as well be happy, for I get plenty palm wine.'

As if by magic, mugs and cups appeared all round the interior of the truck. A youth opposite me began to sing that mournful dirge heard on long mammy-waggon journeys ever since the first of those resilient trucks was conceived:

Ma Mammy done die;
Ma Pappy done die;
When shall I see ma home?
When shall I see ma na-a-a-tive land?
I'll nebbah forget ma home . . .

followed by the chorus, a rousing:

HOME AGAIN, HOME AGAIN
When shall I see ma home?
When shall I see ma na-a-a-tive land?
I'll nebbah forget ma home.

The song had no sooner ended than another voice in the far corner began to sing in a high, piping tone, a much livelier song this time, the singer just a silhouette from where I sat:

Man, he eat de barracuda,
Barracuda eat de bass,
Bass, he eat de little flounder,
'Cause de flounder lower class,

with the chorus resounding triumphantly round the interior of the truck:

'CAUSE DE FLOUNDER LOWER CLASS . . .

and the singer again:

Little flounder eat de sardine,
Dat is nature's little plan,

Sardine eat de little worm
And de little worm eat Man,

AND DE LITTLE WORM EAT MAN.

The drink was making one of the old ladies beside me talkative. In between bouts of singing she chattered non-stop to anyone who cared to listen. From the folds of her ample dress she produced a bottle of can-can. She uncorked it, put the bottle to her mouth, and handed it to me. I took a small sip, feeling the fire within me as the liquor burned its way like molten lava down through my tubes to declare instant war upon my liver. She indicated that I should give Graffish Boy a swig at the bottle.

I lurched over to the old man, not quite sure whether it was the violent swaying of the lorry or the effects of the drink or both that was causing my unsteadiness. He shone the torch to guide me, and by the light of it I saw something laid across his lap that I had not seen for years, something that I instantly recognized as a 'talking stick'. This was a small wand of carved ebony with very short strips of leather attached to the tip, a symbol of authority used by some northern chiefs to wave at their subjects when they wanted absolute silence during meetings and discussions. He readily acquiesed to my request to borrow it for a moment and I returned with it to my seat.

The old mammy was still chattering. I waved the talking stick threateningly at her. The whole mammy-waggon interior exploded with laughter. When the laughter subsided, she chortled, 'Eh, massa, a fit-looking young man like you – you no' get bigger and better stick to show me than that small-small thing?'

Graffish Boy started to sing, his wicked old eyes gleaming in the corner:

> *My little sister work for Lagos,*
> *Dat is why I sing dis song,*
> *White men buy her plenty whisky –*
> *She make money all night long.*

The howls of mirth this time must have disturbed the slumbering monkeys in the surrounding forests as the truck sped on its way, and the refrain was so loud as to seem like splitting the star-lit heavens asunder:

SHE MAKE MONEY ALL NIGHT LONG.

The supply of palm wine and can-can seemed endless. The singing got louder and louder and I was as rowdy as the others. I doubt if there was a happier collection of people in all of Christendom than we as our mammy-waggon, Jear-Box Commander at its helm, thundered on its way through that long and sublimely drunken African night.